From the Barber's Chair

From the Barber's Chair

50th and France Avenue • 1936-1988

*By Vern Swanson
as told to
Tom Clark*

Illustrated by Bob Connolly

NODIN PRESS
Minneapolis

Picture Credits

Alan Bachman, p. 90; Rev. John Benson, p. 60 (bottom); Mrs. Harry W. Casey, p. 97 (top); Marion Danens, pp. 49 (bottom left and middle), 84, 106; Barbara Dennison and Virginia McLain, pp. 88, 89, 91; Edina City Clerk, p. 49 (top right); Edina Courier/Edina Sun, pp. 81, 98, 99, 107; Edina Historical Society, pp. 13, 14, 49 (top left and middle), 67, 70, 76, 81, 82, 87, 92 (bottom), 93 (top and bottom), 94 (top and bottom), 96, 97 (bottom), 100, 101, 103, 109, 110; Edina Public Library, p. 102; Ray Garrison, p. 72; Alberta Hartzell, p. 92 (top); Marie Hedberg, p. 15; C. J. "Connie" Hoigaard, p. 60 (top); Tom Martinson, p. 104; Minneapolis Collection of the Minneapolis Public Library, pp. 26, 74; Minneapolis Star/Tribune, p. 63; Minnesota Historical Society, pp. 32/33, 34, 35 (E. D. Becker), 36, 50 (Jack Gillis, Mpls. Star), 52, 73, 111; Michael Moormann, covers and p. 7; Del Nelson, p. 85; St. Patrick's Church, p. 61 (top and bottom); St. Paul Dispatch/Pioneer Press, p. 36; Vern Swanson, pp. 6, 24, 25, 42, 45, 47, 49 (bottom right), 51, 56

Copyright © 1988 Tom Clark

All rights reserved. No part of this book may be reproduced in any form without the permission of Nodin Press Inc. except for review purposes.

ISBN 0-931714-34-6

Nodin Press, a division of Micawber's, Inc.
525 North Third Street
Minneapolis, MN 55401
Printed in U.S.A., at Gopher State Litho, Minneapolis, MN

To Sid Gunn, who never broke his chain
of haircuts by me from 1936 to 1986.
— *V.C.S*

To my dad, James E. Clark, who taught
me how to listen to people's stories
— *T.W.C.*

More Than Half

1936 Bert Davis stands at his chair, and Vern stands next to customer Kenny Lindgren, bartender at Bob's restaurant next door. This was taken in Bert's barber shop about two years after Vern began cutting hair.

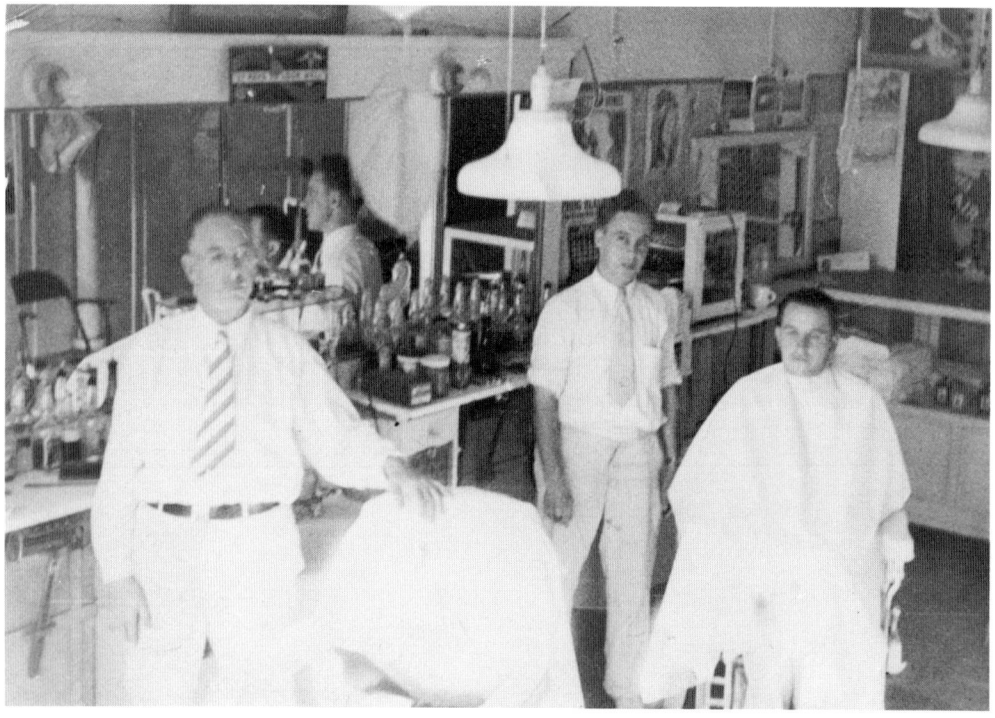

a Century of Barbering

1988 Vern cuts Tom Clark's hair at Edina Barber Shop while they discuss their book.

Contents

PREFACE	11	Lamitz	57
INTRODUCTION	13	The Ice Cream Man	57
Notes	19	Big Gus and Little Gus	58
MY ROOTS	20	Fred Gaulke (Gohlke)	59
Through the Woods	23	Little Erick	59
The Stitching Hole	24	Home Haircuts	59
Bounty Hunting	25	Two Priests	61
The Truck Farm	27	The Bucketts and Trisler	61
THE BARBERSHOP	29	The Painter	63
How It All Began	31	Nelson Brothers	64
Barber School	33	John	64
Little Sisters of the Poor	35	Haeg	65
The Hot Summer of '36	36	Joe Danens	65
First Jobs	37	**PLACES AND EVENTS**	67
Bert's Barber Shop	37	Elgin Creamery	69
The War Impact	38	Edina Theatre	69
Vern's Shop	38	Bowling Alley	71
Apprentices	39	The White Grill	71
Barbering Fifty Years Ago	41	France Avenue	72
A Good Shave	43	Armistice Day Snowstorm	74
The Waiting Room	43	Windstorm of 1950	75
A Child's First Haircut	45	**WALKING TOURS**	77
Shoe-Shine Boys	46	Tour A	79
Later Years at Vern's	46	Tour B	83
PERSONALITIES	49	Tour C	89
The Willsons	51	Tour D	91
The Blacksmiths	53	Tour E	95
Sorenson	55	Tour F	103
George Payne	55	Notes to the Walking Tour	109
Kent	55	**AFTERWORD**	113

Preface

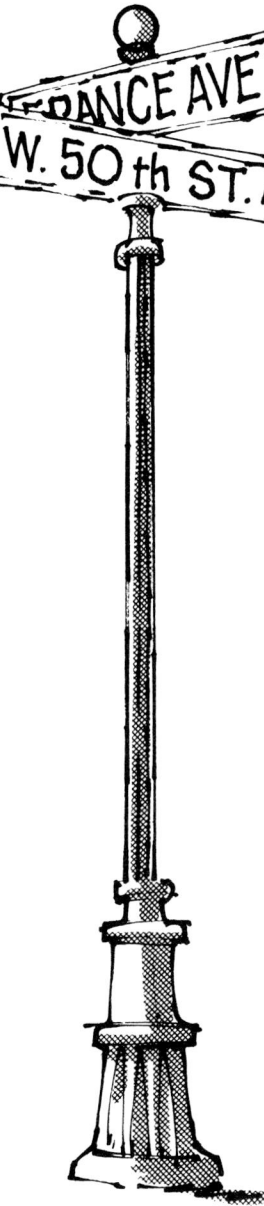

This book about 50th and France in Edina, Minnesota, is primarily oral history, Vern Swanson's memories of the people and shops in the area in the 1930s and 1940s. He remembers the doorways, the counters and the tools as well as the proprietors themselves, many of whom were customers of his barbershop from as far back as August of 1936. He relates stories about his own growing up, he tells about his decision to be a barber, and he describes the changes in the barbering profession over the last half century.

    The reader can also take a walking tour, using as a guide the section that summarizes the history of each building in order. Notes, short sections of bold print and an introduction about the 1920's supply factual details from secondary sources and from interviews with other Edina residents.

    The idea for the book occurred to me late in 1984. I had been a customer of Vern's at the Edina Barber Shop for about ten years when Vern was describing for me one day the lanes of a bowling alley in the basement right below us. The more he talked, the more intrigued I became by the details he remembered and the stories he told. I knew that the *Edina Sun* had written an article about him when he retired from full-time barbering in January of 1980, but now I realized that something longer was waiting to be recorded.

    With Vern's cooperation, I began in January of 1985 to tape record my monthly haircuts. At first these were the standard twenty minutes, but in the last two years they have more often been double and triple that length so that we could talk and record without being rushed. Vern would stand back from the barber chair, scissors in one hand and comb in the other, intent on my question, and begin to reminisce. On three occasions we took hour-long walks to establish the walking tour section.

    All the tapes were transcribed into notebooks, and from an arrangement of these the text has emerged. Sometimes, as in the flowing narrative of Vern's roots, the text is virtually word for word as it was spoken. At other times, Vern has told parts of the same story on separate occasions, and my task was to blend them into a single account. In all the longer anecdotes, it is evident that the stories have been told many times before. As time went along, we verified and honed details of the text in phone calls, notes to each other, and meetings in the shop's backroom. My last step was to verify dates and names and to place Vern's recollections in a context.

Early shaping of the book came from the Edina Writers' Group, especially Joan Schulz, Marilyn Halker, and Ron Balej, who spurred me on to completion. Joan Schulz, in particular, had important insights for changes and additions. My editor, Norton Stillman, knew just how to broaden my vision and challenge my easy solutions. And my design artist, Bob Connolly, has been a sensitive and enthusiastic colleague.

I am grateful to many people for assistance: to my wife, Sue, for encouragement and good judgment; to Donna Skagerberg and Jim Fenlason at the Edina Historical Society, for assistance with research; to Hosmer Brown, Patricia Lund, Marlin Ramler, and First Bank Edina, for typing funds; to Ray Bechtle, for editing suggestions; to Kathy Henkels, for spotting errors and for typing; to Foster Dunwiddy of the Edina Heritage Foundation, for gathering and copying photographs and for on-site analysis of two buildings; to Michael and Mark Moormann, for taking photographs and for drawing the map; to Harold Sand, for source material; to John Baule at the Hennepin County Historical Society, for suggestions and encouragement; to Cynthia Nelson, for strong but gentle editing; and to the many past and present neighbors of 50th and France who have supplied pieces of information.

The account on these pages is a beginning rather than a complete picture, because there are more Edina residents who can provide further pieces for this puzzle of local history. I hope that this beginning will whet a curiosity for more history of the area.

Oral history, which is the systematic recording of oral tradition, was not invented until 1948, halfway through these fifty-plus years of Vern's barbering. The tape recorder appeared fortuitously at a time when letter writing was declining, yet storytellers were still interesting and articulate.* In the best folk tradition, Vern is a storyteller whose dialogue, economy and focus of detail are entertaining. All readers should find human interest in these anecdotes. Friends will recognize his familiar style, and others will discover the genuine and warm gentleman that Vern is.

Tom Clark
December 1987

*See David K. Dunaway and Willa K. Baum, *Oral History* (Nashville, Tennessee, American Association for State and Local History, 1984).

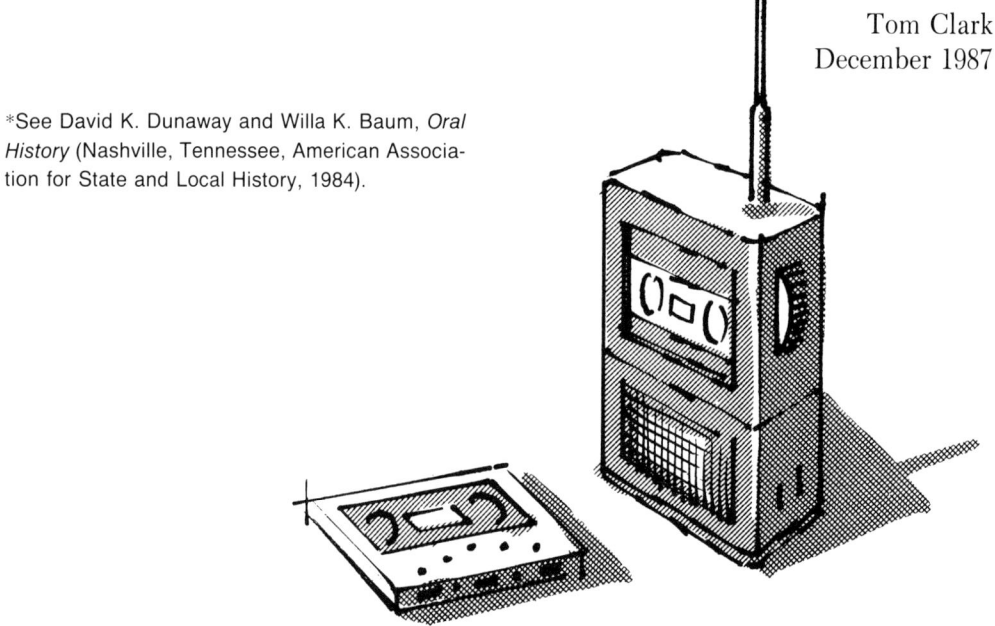

Introduction

West 50th Street and France Avenue are thoroughfares that both date back to at least 1886.[1] Perhaps the presence of Trinity Chapel, one of the earliest Edina buildings that is still standing, helped cause an intersection of two country roads. Trinity Chapel of the Episcopal Church was built in 1872 on what is now the northwest corner of 50th and France. During the 1880s it was converted to a residence.[2]

By ca. 1910, the first two commercial buildings had been built on the corner of 50th and France, the general store on the southwest corner and, a few feet to the west, Lilja's blacksmith shop.[3] Gene Delaney (b. 1909) remembers riding a horse into this shop to have it shoed.[4]

In December of 1913, John Buckett bought the two-story general store from realtors Stevenson and Pearce and moved into the second-floor quarters with his family.[5] He sold feed, kerosene, and hardware, as well as groceries from the Red and White chain. His trade, which was mostly groceries, was with farmers who telephoned their orders in the morning and had them delivered in folding crates in the afternoon.[6]

Albert Nelson, the druggist on the southeast corner of 50th and France, used to tell Gene Delaney how he would stay open for business late on nights when there were dances in the Hartzell garage or on France Avenue by 50th Street. A bulletin announcing a dance would be put out every once in awhile. In the middle twenties, John Buckett

George Hartzell stands in front of his first garage in 1924. The Edina Creamery building is visible at the right. Cement blocks like these can still be seen towards the rear of this building. The gas pumps were worked by hand until up to ten gallons of gas filled a marked tube. Then the hose was pulled down to the car.

Behind George Hartzell's tow truck can be seen the Kell, Oxborough, and Riley residences. The photo was taken from Hartzell's garage on 50th Street ca. 1924.

moved his food business across France Avenue to the location later managed by Knutson and Turner. Harley Winn then became proprietor of the corner hardware store, and he and his wife Grace lived upstairs. Gene Delaney recalls seeing "some devils" go up to the Winns' apartment one night around 1928 or 1929 and lower Grace's piano down onto the street with ropes. Gene had ridden to the dance on horseback, and although he doesn't remember who played the piano that night, he knows it wasn't Grace.[7]

When John Lilja moved his blacksmith trade around the corner to a shop on France Avenue, a Mr. Lundblad and Roy Lockwood built a garage where the first blacksmith shop had been. This was taken over by George Hartzell sometime before 1924.[8] Hartzell's Edina Garage was built of concrete blocks and had a twelve-foot high basement where Grace Hansen (b. 1903) remembers her parents and other Edina residents storing their cars for the winter since the motors wouldn't start anyway.[9]

Vern remembers hearing why Hartzell moved a block away on France Avenue about this time:

> "Hartzell's first garage burnt down, and that was when they moved over there — about 1925. Bert Davis came here in 1924, and he told about the fire. George Krieger, the West (Minneapolis) High School music teacher, had his car in there, and he had just got it out and parked it on the street when the fire come. He told me about that."

And Grace Hansen recalls that the fire rig on its way from 43rd and Upton had trouble at the intersection of 50th and Chowen because of the low, swampy conditions there. A firemen was thrown from the rig and was either injured or killed.[10]

In 1988, the basement at this site retains charred surfaces on many support beams and cement blocks. It appears that, after the Hartzell fire, the cement-block structure of the building and some of the support posts and beams were retained, while new joists, flooring and support posts were added.

The Elgin Creamery had been on 50th Street west of the garage since about 1919.[11] Its first name was the Edina Creamery, and its first owner was a Danish man named Nicholaeszen.[12] By 1921, when part of the operation was run at the Browndale farm, it had the name Lake Harriet Creamery. Gladys Hansen, who was the bookkeeper, met her future husband Christ Hansen at the creamery in the early twenties when he was a partner in the firm. Grace Hansen, her sister, remembers that all the men who worked

Dairy partner Christ Hansen sits on the hood of his Reo delivery truck. An earlier sign on the same truck had the names Brandley and Knudsen.

in the dairy at that time lived in a boarding house across 50th Street and that the lady who ran this house was a good cook. Leslie Buckett (b. 1895) identifies this as Sullivan's rooming house, the Trinity Chapel building. Grace and Gladys Hansen's father and grandfather sold milk to the creamery from their farms between France and Wooddale.[13]

Some of the neighboring farms that brought milk to the creamery were those belonging to Nelson, Wind, Haeg, McCauley, Delaney and Jones.[14] Delivery was made at first by horse-drawn wagons. At the sound of a bell on the wagon, women would come out of their houses with pans and bottles to be filled with milk. By 1921, deliveries began to be made by a Reo truck.[15]

Mrs. Alberta Hartzell (b. 1900) recalls the horse-drawn bobsleds that brought ice up from Lake Calhoun and from the Mill Pond on Minnehaha Creek for use at the creamery. The ice would be packed with sawdust and stored in sheds. She also remembers the water pumps at the creamery in the twenties, the special hand-manipulated brushes for cleaning bottles, and the steam boilers used for sterilizing them. In cold weather, white steam came from the pipes of the bottling plant.[16]

John McCauley remembers being with his father when he brought milk cans to the Elgin Creamery around 1926. The double-lane driveway, whose entrance was on 50th Street, was between the office building on the right and the bottling building on the left as they entered. They would drive up to the steel chute and, when it opened up, would hoist the five- or ten-gallon cans onto the truck-level platform. Inside, the men would pull the cans in and pour the milk into a large vat for pasteurizing.[17]

McCauley also recalls that his father bought dairy cattle from a middleman named Tomboy, whose grassland extended along France Avenue from the newer Hartzell garage to about 45th Street. McCauley and Nelson both have fond remembrances of the popcorn wagon in the 50th and France neighborhood in the 1920s. This horse-drawn wagon had a whistle that could be detected blocks away in the quiet neighborhood. Grace Hansen's father sold popcorn to the wagon's owner who also sold ice cream. It was one of the features of a Sunday afternoon in the "country" for one of John McCauley's uncles to be able to buy a gallon of this ice cream.[18]

Kenneth Krake's father had a "small produce farm next to the dairy where we raised melons, corn, potatoes, dill, tomatoes, cucumbers, etc., and sold fresh vegetables to the neighbors."[19] The Krakes' farmland and small white house were owned by John Hatting.[20] Kenneth also recalls the paving of 50th Street in the late 1920s:

"Our front yard had several huge oak trees and they had to cut them down to widen the street for paving. The trees were cut down with two-man crosscut saws (before the days of chain saws). It was a sad day when they cut down our favorite climbing trees."[21]

In 1927 or 1928, Elgin Creamery, also called Elgin Dairy Products Company, was sold by a Mr. Bankey to Norris Dairy, whose main plant was in Minneapolis on 28th and Emerson.[22] In 1933 or 1934, the bottling building was demolished, but as Vern remembers hearing from Bert Davis, the two-story office building was moved across France Avenue and is the current Bing Plumbers building.[23]

While 50th and France around 1920 still had only three businesses, the corner just six blocks to the north at 44th and France was developing into a commercial hub. It served as a shopping area for residents of Morningside, a suburban division of farmland platted in 1905 and served by streetcars.[24] It was called Westgate, although for a while around 1930 it was also called the Country Club Shopping Area, a name that would later be attached to 50th and France.

It was in the mid-twenties that 50th and France became the shopping area for the Country Club development of realtor Samuel Thorpe, whose lots first went on sale in 1924. His understanding with home owners was that they would rely on their automobiles for transportation.[25]

In 1925, West 50th Street was still a dirt road with occasional houses scattered between the Edina Mill near Wooddale Avenue and the Minneapolis city limits at France Avenue.[26] The 1925 platt map shows that the four houses across 50th Street from the dairy were owned at this time by Harold E. Hineline (the Trinity Chapel residence), Byron E. Kell, W. J. and Effie Oxborough, and Ann N. Riley.

When Vern came to Bert's Barber Shop in 1936, the city directory for the area still included only the residences of the Country Club district. In 1938, the neighborhoods of South Harriet Park (Morningside), Hansen Park, and White Oaks Addition were added. The directory for 1939 includes under the "Metropolitan Area of Edina" the above neighborhoods as well as Colonial Grove, Browndale Park, Thielen's Addition, Rolling Green, and Mirror Lake. But it was not until 1943 that all residences were listed in a unified alphabet.[27]

The Minneapolis neighborhoods on the east side of France around 50th were being built also in the 1920s and 30s. These residents have been customers at the corner from those early times. One Minneapolis business with early origins was Thompson Lumber Company, which opened a branch yard at 50th and Ewing in 1923.[28]

By 1936, one decade after the Hartzell fire and the acres of vegetables and the corner feedstore, Vern began to cut hair in a shop that was one of about three dozen commercial establishments. The change had been fast and dramatic over the previous decade. As yet, most of the shops were still practical: realty, food, drugs, clothing, cars, and various services for cleaning and repairing. Ads in the 1936 local directory sent Edinans to Lake Street or downtown Minneapolis for gifts, books, picture framing, and interior decorating. But even though rural elements remained in 1936, Vern was beginning his career as a barber at the busiest intersection of a blossoming and important suburb.

Notes to the Introduction

1 William W. Scott and Jeffrey A. Hess, *History and Architecture of Edina, Minnesota* (City of Edina, 1981), p. 8.

2 Scott, pp. 60–61

3 Hauck interview of Leslie Buckett et al., February 19, 1970, at the Edina Historical Society.

4 Gene Delaney interview, August 27, 1987.

5 Buckett interview.

6 Buckett interview; Mae Krake interview, November 30, 1986; and Grace Hansen interviews, June 20 and August 2, 1987.

7 Gene Delaney interview.

8 Gene Delaney interview; 1924 picture in the Hartzell file at the Edina Historical Society; and interview with Alberta Hartzell, March 31, 1987.

9 Grace Hansen interview, June 26, 1987.

10 Grace Hansen interview.

11 Alberta Hartzell interview and Buckett interview.

12 Grace Hansen interview. Leslie Buckett states that Nicholaeszen had first a dairy, then a meat market, and then the dairy again. (Buckett interview.)

13 Interviews with Grace Hansen, June 26 and July 10, 1987, and Buckett interview. Glady's maiden and married names were both Hansen.

14 Interviews with Alberta Hartzell (March 31, 1987), Grace Hansen (June 26, and August 2, 1987), and John McCauley (July 10, 1987).

15 Grace Hansen interview, June 26, 1987.

16 Interviews with Alberta Hartzell, March 31, April 6, and April 11, 1987.

17 John McCauley interview.

18 John McCauley interview and Grace Hansen interview.

19 Letter from Kenneth Krake to the Edina Historical Society, August 22, 1985.

20 Mae Krake interview and 1925 platt map (Edina City Hall).

21 Kenneth Krake letter.

22 Interview with Mavis Packard, March 23, 1987. Grace Hansen remembers that the Elgin and Norris names were both part of mergers with larger Minneapolis dairies.

23 This is corroborated by Arnold Bing (b. 1890), who remembers that the building was purchased for $100 and cost $500 to move. (Interview with Heidi Bing, June 22, 1987.)

24 Scott, pp. 10 and 11.

25 Scott, p. 14.

26 Kenneth Krake letter and 1925 platt map.

27 The "Metropolitan" area was "north of 58th and east of Normandale Road; north of 54th and east of Blake Road." Tracy Avenue and Valley View phone numbers were first listed in 1947 when these addresses were given as Minneapolis Route 2.

28 Interview with Scott Ryerse, March 14, 1987.

Carl Swanson's farm near Henry, South Dakota, 1911.

My Roots

Through the Woods

My mother, Alma, was born in Eagle Bend, Minnesota, and her folks, Marion and Naomi Crider, came from Kentucky. When I went back to Kentucky to look up where my grandfather came from, the relatives took us to a location near Ivel. And we walked up into the cemetery, up the side of a mountain two blocks that you couldn't get to with a car. My cousin had brothers, sisters and father and mother that were buried there. There was probably forty, forty-five graves up there. Some of them was whole families. And I said to the cousin, "What was all this?"

And he said, "It was a plague that took all these people in the 1800s and wiped out whole families."

My grandfather was born in 1856. He married at the age of nineteen, at Dassel, Minnesota. Then he cut his way through the woods from Dassel to Eagle Bend with a team of oxen in 1879. My aunt was six weeks old — she was the oldest in the family. Then he homesteaded up there.

And my mother tells about when she was a little girl, her father got a toothache in the dead of winter — cold, blizzard. He finally got on snowshoes and walked twenty miles to the dentist in Long Prairie. He got his tooth pulled, and they broke his jawbone. Then he had to walk home through the woods on snowshoes again for another three days with the pain of that.

The Stitching Hole

My father, Carl, was born on Girard Avenue North in Minneapolis. His father was sixteen years old when he came from Sweden with his father.

My father always told about my grandfather who, when he was sixteen years old, was walking behind a lumber wagon on Nicollet Avenue. He was following behind the wagon, and his dad told him, "Why don't you get up on the sidewalk? You look like a dog back there."

"Well," my grandfather says, "I thought the sidewalk was for the American people." I think he was just kiddin'. I think he knew.

My father went out to Henry, South Dakota, with his folks. He learned to be a harness maker when he was sixteen years old. Every Saturday night when he got paid, my grandfather was in to collect my father's wages. And my father got pretty sick and tired of that. So they always had an old "stitching horse" where they put needles, and in the bottom of that—in the stitching hole—he put a dollar or two every Saturday night before his old man got the paycheck. Then, when he had accumulated enough in there to buy his ticket to Minneapolis, he hopped on the train. In Minneapolis, he turned right around and called his folks and told 'em where he was. So he wasn't a runaway.

Then he got a job working in a St. Paul harness shop called Scheffer and Rosins. After he worked there a few years, he met my mother. A little later he quit his harness job for lack of horses—machinery had come in. So he left there and went off to South Dakota where he took up a 420-acre homestead in 1910. He and my mother used to write back and forth. Then two years later, they got married in Minneapolis and went back to South Dakota.

Scheffer and Rosins harness factory in St. Paul, ca. 1904. Vern's dad is at the front right. The stitching horse in the lower foreground had clamps for holding leather taut while a waxed thread was brought through with an awl.

Vern holds the reins of Pete, the horse he and Kenneth rode to school. In this photo from ca. 1924, Vern's sister Helen and brother Bill (far right) have posed with them.

Bounty Hunting

A mile and a half from us was a one-room schoolhouse. One teacher had forty kids in all subjects, all eight grades. Five miles away in Henry, the school had maybe ten or twelve rooms. A math teacher would teach math to all the grades, but that's all she'd have to teach.

My father thought we'd have better schools if we'd go to town to school. So my brother and I rode horseback five miles to school and five miles home night and morning.

When I was ten and my brother was seven, we used to set pocket-gopher traps on the way to and from school. At noon we'd take and go up to the county auditor, whose name was Walsh, and we'd pull our pocket-gopher tails and feet out of our pockets and hand 'em to him. He would look at 'em and he'd say, "Lay 'em right over there," which was the window seat. He didn't want to handle them in his hands, and I don't blame him. So he'd pay us ten cents apiece for them, and then we'd go up to the confectionery store and buy our lunch with the money.

One time my lunch wasn't so good, but I had two slices of bread. So I went into the butcher shop, and I asked the butcher if I could buy two cents worth of minced ham. He said, "I don't really know how to slice this," but then he sliced off a couple slices and gave it to us.

Farmers Market on 2nd Avenue North and 7th Street in Minneapolis in the 1930s. Each farmer had ten or twelve feet to display and sell.

The Truck Farm

On the truck farm in South Dakota, they had seven crop failures, one after another from 1920 till 1927. In 1927, my father had an auction sale and sold the farm. We beat it out of there and came to Robbinsdale to a twenty-acre truck farm.

My brother and I grumbled, you know, because we had to work. So my dad used to say to us, "You won't have to work all day when we get this truck farm — you can go out after supper and work on the hoe." And he was right . . . we went out after supper on the hoe, but we worked all day too!

We had probably some one thousand tomato plants. We had a couple acres of strawberry. We had cucumbers and cabbage too. We used to pick cucumbers and haul 'em down to the Gedney pickle factory on Lowry Avenue, and they'd buy all you'd take down there. When you pick cucumbers, if you get the ones that are pickles today, the day after tomorrow they'll be slicers. They grow that fast.

I remember my father saying that there was a blind man down at the market who used to come through selling newspapers. He was always kidding that he was going to get that blind man out here to pick cucumbers because he thought he'd pick 'em cleaner than we did. And if some of my friends would come over when I was picking cucumbers, he'd tell us, "One boy is a boy. Two boys is half a boy. And three boys is no boy at all, so you fellows better run off home!" He got quite a kick out of that.

We had a stall in the vegetable market, which was on 2nd Avenue North and 7th Street. It was the #338 stall. I remember we'd be up at 4 A.M., be down there at quarter to six in the morning, and have our stuff laid out, ready to sell. The grocery men would walk through there. They'd see something they wanted, and they'd stop and buy it. But we couldn't carry over from our truck to the grocery man's truck until six A.M.

In those days, you know, the grocers all went down to the market to buy their vegetables and take 'em back to their stores to sell 'em. Now the farmers' market is pretty much all gone.

On the farm we had three or four cows, and my dad would get a dozen hogs. We'd feed the hogs cabbage leaves and carrot tops until fall. Then he'd throw corn into 'em for about six weeks before he butchered 'em, and that would firm up the meat.

Of course, we didn't have freezers then. We had ice boxes. So my mother had to can the meat. She cold-packed the pork in fruit jars, put water into a boiler, set the glass jars on a piece of wood in the boiler, boiled it probably two hours, took 'em out of there, screwed the caps tight, set 'em up, and let 'em cool off. Then we had meat in the winter, and she would make gravy out of the juice.

They would also cut pork chops, fry 'em, and bury 'em in their own lard in a twelve-gallon crock in the basement so that flies couldn't get at it. As you needed 'em, you'd go down there and dig 'em out, bring 'em up and warm 'em up on the stove. They were ready to serve.

The Barbershop

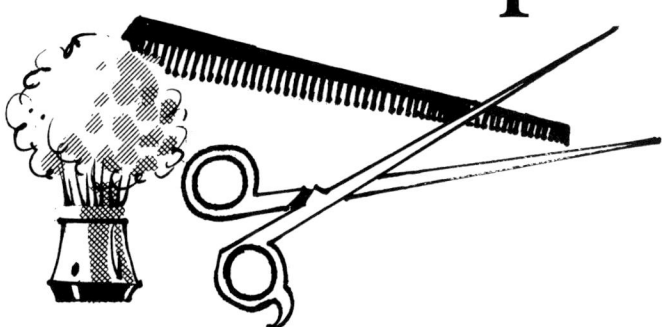

How It All Began

About six months before I went to barber school, I cut my brother's hair. He was seventeen years old, and I was twenty-one. The more I cut, the worse it got. Even though there was a hot spell, he had to wear his earlappers down, it was so bad.

I can remember him going like that over to Robbinsdale school to get some scraps for our hogs. We had cabbages and tomatoes on our truck farm, and the trimmings went into a basket for the hogs. Then if there wasn't enough trimmings, we'd have to pick weeds for them or we'd go over to the school, sort through the trash barrels and shake out the crusts of bread or bits of sandwiches and feed them to the hogs. Nobody saw him with his earlappers that day, but he was afraid they would.

I think my father fixed that haircut for him. He was the one that used to cut our hair. As a matter of fact, I never saw the inside of a barbershop until I was sixteen years old. My father would set us up on the rainbarrel and use a hand clippers. I used to think he took the clippers away from our heads before he was done. Later on, I learned that if you squeeze the clippers and oscillate the blades, they will go back open as you release it so that it doesn't pull the hair.

Then, when I was sixteen, my mother used to take us down to a barbershop once in a while, and I'd go in there and talk to those guys. And there were two barber colleges that I would go by, down in the Gateway district near the Farmer's Market. These were Moser and Twin City. I always thought I wanted to be a barber. But my brother always used to say that his haircut was why I had to go to barber school.

I was working for Schaeffer Refrigerator in the fall of 1935, and I got laid off. On the way home to Robbinsdale on the streetcar, I met a young friend of mine who said, "I bet you don't know what I done today."

"No," I says. "I don't know."

I started barber school!"

I says, "What? You know, that's something that I always wanted to do and never could get in on it. Cost money to go there, and I can never get the money to go."

"Well," he says, "I didn't either. So I went down there with twenty-five dollars, and they let me buy the tools for twenty-five dollars. The rest I worked out in custodial work — sweeping floors, and cleaning spittons, and scrubbin' floors."

So I says, "I wonder if they could use any more?"

And he says, "Why don't you come and try?"

The next morning there I was down at 212 Hennepin with twenty-five dollars I had borrowed from my dad, and poundin' on the door of Twin City Barber College. Doc Gilsdorf, the owner and manager, says, "We could use one more." I started there, and I put in my thousand hours.

Graduates of the Twin City Barber College on Hennepin Avenue pose in 1922 with their instructors.

Barber School

I sat on the stool in the back of the barber school for half a day stropping an old razor on a block of wood to get the swing and rhythm of how they do it. Then the next day they moved me up on the chair.

The twenty-five dollars you paid for the tools included a hand clipper and a pair of shears and two razors. They'd give you an idea what to do with the clippers, and then the first few haircuts that you done were free. After you got so customers didn't have to screw their hat on or the wind would blow it off, then the college got a dime for it. After you were in school for about two months, your haircuts were fifteen cents from then on until the time you got out of school.

The customers were mostly transients that lived around Gateway Park. Some of them, I remember, stayed at Reverend Paul's Union City Mission. And families would bring their kids down too.

We had class every morning from eight o'clock until nine. We had to study the

Fifth from the right is Vern's instructor, Doc Gilsdorf.

Gateway District in Minneapolis, seen from an upper floor of the Nicollet Hotel. Twin Cities Barber College is to the left on the first floor of the Phoenix Hotel.

whole human anatomy—the muscles and nerves, the digestive system, the outer layers of the skin, the scalp. Never used any of that except that you'd kind of recognize what you saw.

One time later in my shop, I had a fella come in to me and he says, "I got somethin' when I was in here last time."

I says, "What was that?"

"Cirrhosis."

"No," I says. "You didn't get cirrhosis. You got psoriasis, and you didn't get that here. That comes from your own mechanical make-up in your body."

But, you know, that psoriasis is so bad that at times I've had customers that had to go to the hospital for a week and sit under a light to dry it up. Then they'd control it a little bit with a yellow ointment. But it'd still grow back a little worse and a little worse, and after maybe another year they'd have to go back and do the same thing over.

Then we'd go up and do practice work until six o'clock. There were about fifty of us men, and there were two ladies. The fellow that owned the school we never liked to have come and look at our haircut because we spent time on it and we tried to do as well as we could, and he'd come along, pick it up and ruin everything that we did.

Whenever you finished a haircut that you felt was a finished product, you would wait for the other instructor, Bob Hunter, to see if you couldn't beckon him over to look at it. 'Cause he'd come over, and if it was passable, why he'd say, "That's fine. Go ahead." And if it wasn't, he'd show you where you were wrong.

One time I was cuttin' a guy's hair, and Bob came along. He walked behind me and said, "You'd better quit now before you spoil it." In other words, I was through and didn't know it.

But old Doc Gilsdorf, the owner, was a better shaver than he was a hair cutter. In his day, shaving was the art. He had a record that he could shave a man in a minute and a half. He might cut his chin off, but that was the way he did it. He'd show you how, and if he cut the guy, he'd hand you the razor and walk away. It was your baby now!

Little Sisters of the Poor

After you got in enough time at the barber school, you could practice at the Little Sisters of the Poor. Our instructors picked two of us, and we went once a week.

We had twenty-five shaves apiece to do, and we had two and a half, three hours to do 'em in. But we never used any steam towels and we never used any hot towels and we never shaved a second time over — usually you shaved a person twice. This way, the instructor at the barber school had a solution that he mixed to soften the beard up — wherever he got it, I don't know, but he made it himself. It was a liquid, and I remember it was green. You'd take some of that liquid in the palm of your hand and rub it into the fellow's beard. You'd just take your lather brush and lather it up and strop your razor and hoe 'im off. As soon as you were done shaving 'im, you took a towel, wiped his face, set 'im up, and off he went. You didn't shave his neck or anything.

The sisters were good to those people, and they were very nice to us. They let us in, and then we went about our business. The only section we got into was where the men were. They had two barber chairs there, so that each of us had a chair.

There was some that were bedridden, and when they got that far, they didn't want to be shaved. But the sister that was there, she'd say, "He doesn't know what he wants." So for his appearance when his people came to see 'im, why he should look nice. So you'd have to go in and shave 'im. It was kind of cruel: you'd have to hold down his arm with your elbow!

That was some of the best training one could ever get — shaving those fellows — because they were old and had a hard beard. I used what they called a double duck razor, made in Germany. That was the best razor I ever had. And we had an old fella at Little Sisters of the Poor that was ninety-seven years old. He was a fireman from out at Anoka. Everytime I come in there, he'd say, "Use the duck!" 'cause that didn't pull his beard.

For a while they still made that razor, but it went into the hands of a different company. They still called it the double duck, but it wasn't the same razor it had been. This here one that I had finally seemed to lose its temper. I'd hold it, and it wasn't there. I thought, "Well, I'll send it in and get it reground and see what comes back." So when it came back, I tried to use it, but the temper was all gone. I gave it to my daughter who put it in a shadow box, a shelf with pigeon holes in it. She wanted it as a keepsake — my first razor along with my dad's razor because he always shaved with a straight edge.

Twin Cities residents slept in the parks because of the heat in July of 1936. The scene above is a St. Paul park.

The Hot Summer of '36

That summer of '36 had record heat — 108°. When I'd take the streetcar down to the barber school, I'd walk through Dayton's because that was about the only place that was air conditioned. And when I was walking down Nicollet Avenue to the school, I'd hear ambulances going by with the people who had collapsed from the heat. I'd see the police going along Gateway Park and poking with a cane the transients who were laying around on the grass. If they didn't move, they were brought down to cots in the old armory because the hospitals were full. It was so hot, a lot of students from the barber college would go up to Loring Park and lay on the grass all night. Everywhere you looked, there were people with pillows.

Every weekday morning that summer, I was at 9th and Nicollet to polish a brass sign on the window ledge which read, "Phillip's Millinery." Every weekday at noon, I returned to the same store to raise the awning and sweep the sidewalk. My wage for this was $2.50 per week. I earned an additional $2.50 a week by going to the Little Sisters of the Poor and doing twenty-five shaves.

And I'll never forget the time in barber school when my dad came in for a haircut. I cut his hair, and when we were through we went and had coffee, and he gave me five dollars to buy a pair of shoes. But I didn't tell the other students that this was my dad, and they thought he had tipped me five dollars! I guess I was as independent as a hog on ice.

First Jobs

In 1936, I took the State Board examination and got a license as an apprentice. That cost two dollars. Then I went out on East 54th Street; twenty-five-cent haircuts, and I made twelve and a half cents on each one. The biggest week I had was Easter week. I made twelve dollars and I worked from seven o'clock in the morning until nine o'clock at night.

And at that time I drove a Model T Ford. I had to go clear out to Robbinsdale in it. After six weeks, I left there and filled in for two weeks while the barber in Robbinsdale was on vacation. Then I went out to Rockford, Minnesota, where the haircuts were forty cents. And at the end of two weeks, I says to the owner of the barbershop, "You give me ten dollars a week with board and room, and I'll stay."

"Boy, I'd like to," he says, "but I just can't."

So I came back to Minneapolis on August 10th of 1936 and went down to the barber school to see what was available. "Well," they said, "a call came in from 50th and France. Bert Davis."

I says, "I'll talk to 'im."

Bert says, "I wanted to hire a master barber rather than an apprentice, but I'll think it over. Call the school tomorrow morning." So I went on home. Next morning I went on down to the school. They said Bert had called and wanted me to come out and work.

Bert's Barbershop

Bert Davis at 5009 France was the first barber on this corner. He came in 1924, just a short time before Archie Peterson moved up here from 44th and France. Archie was Bert's competition.

One thing I used to hear about from Bert was the Edina baseball team that played out here from 1927 to 1929. Bert was the umpire, and they used to get pretty mad at him sometimes — at the decisions that he made. But there was always a group of players like Sylvester McNellis that was here to protect old Bert.

In 1938, across France Avenue from Bert's, there was a man named Bill Hunt who did radio repair in the back of a building. A year later they rented the front half for refrigerator and appliance sales. Then when the appliances moved out, Bill asked me to come in and start a barbershop in the front of his store. But I said, "I couldn't move across the street from Bert and start another barbershop!" So I didn't, but it was only three or four weeks before a shop started up there which was the Edina Barber Shop. It was started by a fellow by the name of Joe Barnes — and I had a chance to start that!

Before 1938, they didn't have what they call the State Code. In '38, every shop in the whole state of Minnesota had to charge a minimum of fifty cents for a haircut, but they could go as high as they wanted. And they had a guarantee on the apprentice of fifteen dollars a week and, for a master barber, eighteen dollars a week. In those years, the most I earned was twenty-seven dollars a week.

Then, in 1942, I saw an ad by DuPont for help out at Rosemount to build a munitions plant for gunpowder. As far as I know, they never got it into operation, and the University of Minnesota has it now. But I went out there and worked as a common laborer for ninety-eight cents an hour, and in six months I had saved two hundred dollars.

By now, Bert was fifty-nine. He was having trouble with his legs and was trying to move out to California. He wanted $600 for the shop.* But one of my customers said, "Throw the $200 in his lap and see if he takes it." He took it. He went off to California while I carried on the shop.

*Barbers lease space in a building but own their own equipment and furnishings. To them, the "shop" is everything, including the sinks, that isn't nailed to the walls.

The War Impact

Not long after I took over the shop, I had to take a physical at Fort Snelling for entering the service. But I was twenty-eight years old, and they stopped at twenty-six years. Then, towards the end of 1944, I had a high number in the draft, and the government said I either had to go into the army or do essential work. I had two kids, so I applied at Honeywell for turret lathe work. At first I had the day shift from 7 A.M. to 3 P.M. and I would rush home, take a shower and then scoot down to my shop from 3:30 to 6 P.M. for a few haircuts, and that way I kept the place open and paid the rent. Then later I got the shift from 11 P.M. to 7 A.M., and I'd go home, have a glass of warm milk and sleep until just before 3:30 in the afternoon. The work was seven days a week, but that lasted just six months until the war was over.

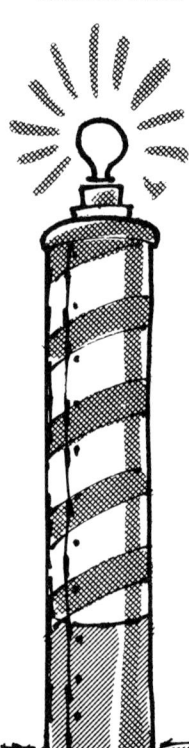

Vern's Shop

When I came in 1936, there was a barber pole attached to the building, and one end of it was set on the sidewalk. It was nothing more at that time than a hot water pressure tank. No hot water in it — just the carcass. Bert had the tank from Big Gus the plumber, and he had the painter on the corner stripe it and then put a light bulb on top. By 1952 or 1953, when I took it down, I bought a new barber pole and attached it to the building. It's up in my garage now. I saved one barber chair and the pole, and I turn the pole on sometimes — it still works.

In those early days before air conditioning, we had to put a hair cloth around our customers and put talcum powder all around the neck of the hair cloth. Then these people would perspire so much that, when we took the cloth off, it was just like mud. This paste would slide from their necks onto the hair cloth. I'd have to put cold water on their necks so I could send 'em out dry. And when the weather got real hot, people were reluctant to come in for a haircut.

But after we got an air conditioner in the transom in about 1959, that was really great! But the barbers working for me wanted the door open for fresh air even though the air conditioner was bringing it in. When I'd leave, they would open the door.

Next to my shop for years there was an empty lot to the south, a hole probably six or seven feet down from the sidewalk. There was a wooden fence across it at the sidewalk. Somebody said I could've bought it for $1800. I used to stand out there and look at that lot. I thought, "Boy, if a guy could buy that, he could build a barbershop and make a good one!" If I'd known then what I know now, I would beg, borrow, or steal to get that lot. But it's down the drain. Oscar Bergerson came along in about 1954 and built the Donuteria.*

A customer of mine, Sid Gunn, used to work for Northern States Power. He would stop every day I was there, and if I wasn't busy we would go next door to the Donuteria. After a while, Walsh and his wife put in a coffee urn, and people could sit down in there.

Sid is my oldest customer — I've cut his hair since 1936. One time, he went away on a vacation where he was with somebody that went to get a haircut. So he went along, and they thought that he might as well get a haircut as long as he was there. Then the barber says, "Do you want to get a haircut, too?" "No!" he says, "It'd spoil my record. Nobody else has ever cut my hair!"

*The first tenant was Korst Jewelry. When Korst moved over to 50th Street in 1957, it became Bear Record Shop until Bob Walsh, the eye doctor's son, took it over as the Donuteria in 1960.

Apprentices

I'll never forget, when I came out here — I was an apprentice, and Nelson the druggist was as bald as a sink. All he had was just around the edge. It took me six minutes to cut his hair. There was nothing more to do. When I got all through and he left, why Bert says, "Don't *ever* do that! Play around some way and kill twenty minutes." So the next time that I got him, I played around for twenty minutes. At least he felt better.

My worst haircut was in the early 1940s. One time I picked up a thinning shear and was gonna thin, and I grabbed the wrong one. I grabbed a regular shears and made a cut that was a big gouge. So I worked long and hard to get that outta there, but I got it out. The customer never knew about it, but for a second it made my heart sink clear to my boots.

Later on, when I was hiring a barber, I always wanted to get an apprentice rather than an experienced barber because you could partially train 'im in the way you wanted 'im. When you'd get somebody that'd been working for somebody else, why they had done that same thing. Well, you didn't always go along with it.

So I used to call both barber colleges in Minneapolis to get students. Then I'd go down and talk to the boy beforehand and have him come out, spend a couple hours and look around. It worked out effectively. I liked it.

The first thing that I looked for in an apprentice was appearance. How they took care of themselves let you know how they would come out with somebody else's hair. And there never was in our shop profanity or smutty stories, so I looked at that. And then after you talked to him for maybe half an hour, you got a pretty good sense of his attitude. 'Cause so many of those kids coming outta school, why they teach 'em in school that they're really going to make a lot of money when they get out there. They forget that they've gotta be there for a year or a year and a half before they can work up the clientele to do that.

The best barber you can have is a navy barber. Why? The practice that they had while they were in the navy. The speed. When they come back here to barber, they still have to go to school to get their license. And they got to slow down, but it gives them a little more time to do the finished product.

You see, you rough-cut a man's hair in ten minutes. Then you wet it and dry it and spend the rest of the time with spots that you see that need your attention.

One time, though, I had an apprentice barber working for me. And Sy Ryan, who built the bowling alley, would come in and get a shampoo. In those days they'd sit in a chair in front of the sink. So this apprentice shampooed his hair and rinsed it out, and then he told Sy, "Now you get back in the barber chair." Well, Sy got out of that chair, and he was trying to feel his way back into the other chair with water running all over his face. I was so embarassed! After that I told the kid, "Don't *ever* do that!"

Barbering Fifty Years Ago

In 1936, the shop had two chairs. They had metal arms that were plated with porcelain so that when they became dirty, you could wash them off. The foot rests were metal on one side, and they turned so that you had upholstery on the back side. When you laid a man down and shaved him, his pants lay on the upholstered side rather than on the dark metal side.

The razor strop I still got. I had this same one fifty years ago in school. It was part of the original equipment I bought. In those days, people got shaves in the barber shop. And we used more cloth towels. When you wrang a towel out, you first laid it on the inside of your arm. If it was too hot there, it was too hot for the face. You would stretch it out and lay it across the mustache, or you would drape it down, fold it up over his cheeks and then lay it on his forehead. There was a bin behind the chairs that we'd throw the towels in after we used 'em, and it was lined with tin because the towels were wet. Then the American Linen truck would come and pick up our linen and bring back what we sent before.

For haircuts, you'd tuck the towel in the collar of the smock, and then fold it over. The paper neck strips at that time were used just for kids. Then back when the Minnesota Gophers were number one in '43 and '44, they had maroon and gold. So we got maroon smocks trimmed in gold.

In those days, you didn't have the hair styling that you have now. It was the conventional haircut. You'd vary from that a little bit whether it was shorter or longer, but the hair never came over the ears. If it came over the ears, it was time to get a haircut. Mustaches were no extra charge, the same as today. But there were no beards until the '60s.

When you go back to 1936, they had a thinning shear that had teeth on both sides. Later they had one with teeth on just one side like we have now, but there weren't as many teeth and the teeth were wider apart. We used 'em some, but they would always show where you took it out. So you had to be very careful. Now in 1972, they came out with what they called a 44/20. That's the number of teeth on the comb (44) and the number to the inch (20). It's more effective, and it acts as a tapering shear.

41

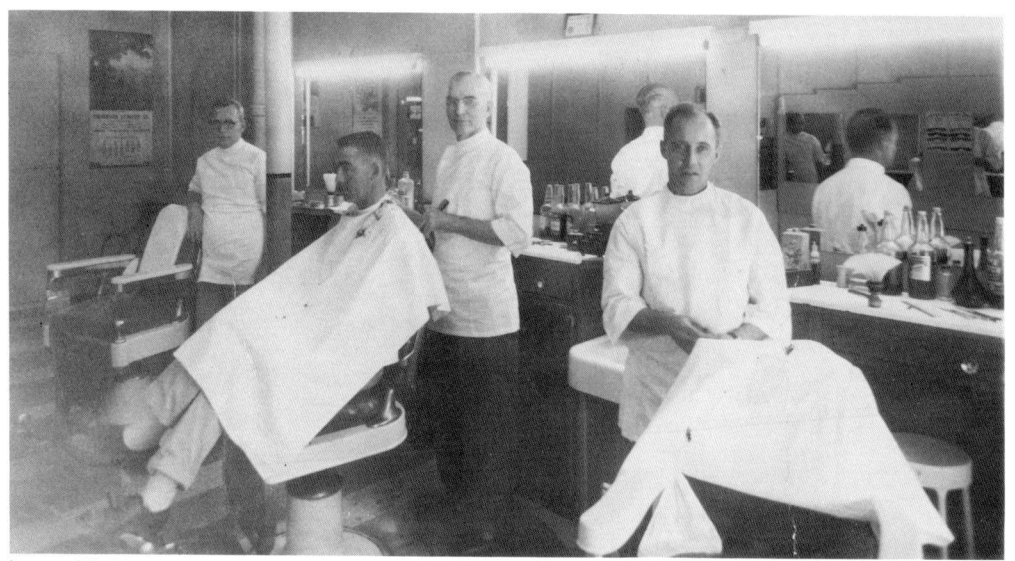

Leroy Hinkle (left) and Vern stand by their chairs while Harry Lind cuts Bill Moynihan's hair in the early 1950s. Bill was a building contractor in Edina.

What looks like a grille in the barbershop picture (page 56) is just a door with a glass window, but they've put paper on the glass so that you didn't see through. It was the door that went down the hall to the bathroom, but the door was only about a foot and a half wide—a big man would have to turn sideways to get through.

Along the wall of the shop was a white marble shelf, about an inch thick and a foot wide, that held all the bottles and other things. When I closed the shop one shelf went to the dump and one shelf I kept. I look at it now and think I should throw it away.

On the shelf in the picture there, you can see Bert's lather machine. This was the first time I ever used one; they just came out. They were made right over here on East Hennepin. They were more sanitary for shaving than lather brushes because you just put your hand under there and scooped up the lather. With the brushes, you used the same brush on everybody's face.

The tonic bottles were there just because the tonic smelled nice. Some kids liked perfume, and some of 'em didn't. Now they wouldn't appreciate it.

Around 1938, there was a retarded man about thirty years old. Sometimes he'd walk into the shop, and he'd come over to the shelf and pick up the tonic bottles. He'd pour tonic over his head to smell nice. But one time he got the Fitch shampoo by mistake—got it down in his eyes. And he never, ever came back to the shop. That was the end of it.

One time a fellow says to me, "Don't put that stuff in my hair. When I go home, my wife will think I've been in a whorehouse." The guy in the next chair says, "Put it on my hair. My wife doesn't know what it smells like in a whorehouse!"

I had two tonic bottles that now would be probably a hundred years old. They were in Bert's shop when I came. They were round and oblong and a dark blue, so dark that you thought it was purple. The stopper on the top was a cork that had a metal straw about two inches long—an inch of it through the cork and an inch of it out the top. The bottle could be up-ended to shake out just the amount of fluid you needed. But I didn't trust the cork to stay on, so I'd hold the edge of it with my thumb when I shook the bottle upside down.

Then I had them set up in the basement of an apartment I owned, but one day somebody walked off with 'em. Once in the late '40s, I was offered ten dollars apiece for them—*then*. To me, they were priceless.

A Good Shave

When I came out here, some of the people would shave themselves, but some of them would come in to the barbershop once a week for a shave.* During World War I, they issued the soldiers safety razors. When the war was over, those boys were used to shaving themselves, so they continued using safety razors at home. That really hurt the barber shaving.

When World War II came along was about the time that the electric razor came out. And that finished it off. There was just a few of those around that wasn't in World War I or II and couldn't shave themselves—you could almost count 'em on your fingers.

When you shaved a man, you shaved the neck too. But you know—you went out into the country, and ninety percent of the people there shaved their necks round. In town here, there was ten percent that shaved like this; here in the city, you shaved down the sides.

I still shave the neck of a couple of my customers. Jimmy Burns is one of 'em. He used to write sports articles for the Tribune. All of the high school kids knew him. He has muscular dystrophy. When his wife died two or three years ago, I think that took an awful lot out of him.

The Waiting Room

Before they had comic books, there was a sewer pipe that came from the apartments above the barbershop. The pipe came right down to the shop through the floor. And I'd get kids in there waiting for haircuts after school, and they were full 'a vinegar. So I'd give the kids a nickel if they shinnied that pole and made it to the ceiling.

Well, it was twelve feet from the floor to the ceiling, and cast iron don't have much grab to it. The kids would pull and push and shove—everything that they could to get up there. Then they'd run out of gas and slide down. I don't think there were probably two or three of 'em that ever made it. They worked pretty hard on it.

And I had kids wrestling on the floor, down around my feet. They had to do something!

*The origin of the word barber (Latin *barba* = beard) links the service to shaves earlier than to haircuts.

Then in the early forties comic books started coming in. I tried to pick out something that was a little realistic, classics like *Robin Hood* and *The Three Musketeers*.

For the grownups, I had *Field and Stream, Look, Life, Saturday Evening Post* and *Reader's Digest*. I like *Reader's Digest* even yet today. And then we had the *Minneapolis Journal*. I remember cartoons there like Andy Gump, terrible tempered Mr. Bang, Toonerville Trolley, and Jubilee's Partner, who was always getting in some kind of a jam.

And we had jackpots before the state in the fifties came out and said that was illegal. We had numbers from one to ten at a dollar apiece, for Millers baseball and U of M football.

But I remember one afternoon about 1942 or 1943 when I was workin' alone. It was after school, and I looked out and counted thirteen kids waiting for haircuts. Almost all haircuts for kids then were "heines" (flat tops). So I thought, "Boy, that's quite a job. I'll forget how to cut a regular haircut." My father-in-law would have said, "I wish I was home and my dog was here."

A Child's First Haircut

When you get a little child in the chair, you don't go at 'im with the full product right away. If I can get 'em in the barber chair, why then I pick up my comb, and I comb their hair for a while first. Then I'll explain to 'em, "We don't want to get all this loose hair all over your clothing. Let's put the cloth on." Usually then they'll let you put that on.

Then I keep combing their hair. And then I pick up the scissors, cut a little bit off the top. And then I keep the comb in my left hand and, after they get immune to that, I reach back and I keep combing while I pick up the clipper. I lay it in back of the chair, and I keep combing as the clipper is humming. Then I'll work it up, a bit at a time, and when they get immune to that, I can bring it up and I can take a little bit off with the clipper.

Once in a while you have somebody that gives you a bad time crying and carrying on. What worried me more than anything was the scissors. I always tried to hold my shears so that any turn would bump them up so the child wouldn't be cut. Children's eyes are precious—you have to be doubly careful!

Vern with a first haircut ca. 1975.

Shoe-shine Boys

Sometimes I would have a shoe-shine boy in the shop. One of the boys, who lived right there in that block, used to shine shoes for me for four or five years. He got free rent, and all he had to do was sit there. He'd pull out a chair. In the wintertime it wasn't so bad, but in the summer kids like to play. We used to give them a little time off. But then when he was fourteen, why he lost interest. Kids are kids.

I had other boys in too. One time, when I had a black shoe-shine boy, I was cutting' a little boy's hair, and I suppose the little boy was four years old. He kept looking at the black shoe-shine boy, and everything was quiet. Then pretty soon, out of the blue sky, this little kid says, "You look just like a nigger!"

The black boy says, "If you was a little bigger, I'd whip ya!"

Kids that age, you know, speak their mind. But I tell you, I bet I turned six colors!

Later Years at Vern's

After the war, I worked alone for four years, and then I got so busy I couldn't handle it. I was on my feet all day, particularly on Saturdays, from eight in the morning until six. I'd sit on the window ledge to grab a bit of sandwich and a swig of coffee to keep my body going. One Saturday, I was so tired I couldn't put one foot in front of the other. So I hired a man by the name of Harry Lind. He lived out here in Edina, and he was the grandest old man that I could have ever saw. He worked for me for twelve years. We never had a cross word all the time that he was here. In October of 1960, he had a stroke, and by Christmas he was gone.

Barbers have trouble with their legs — varicose veins and so on — because of all the standing. I saved mine by using a swivel seat for fifteen years. It was like a bicycle seat that attached to the base of the barber chair with two brackets, and I could go three-fourths of the way around. Nowadays that type of seat won't work because the chair foundations aren't heavy enough.

> In those years there were three barber shops on the corner: Archie Peterson on 50th Street, and Joe Barnes and Vern across the street from each other on France Avenue. The next owners of Archie's shop were Red Kresser and Joe Dietz. When Joe Dietz was ready to sell in 1967, Marty bought his business, which has since been moved next door to the corner location.

Back in 1938, Joe Barnes didn't have a master license, so he couldn't open a barbershop. There was another man who worked with him for two or three years. Then Joe got his master license and carried on.

The Edina Barber Shop, after Joe sold out around 1942, changed hands as many as six or seven times before Jack Carter bought it. They were all fine men — all of 'em. I liked 'em all. They were good competition. They were honest, and we always enjoyed each other. Fact is, when I worked alone, why we switched haircuts. They'd come over and I'd cut their hair, and then I'd go over there and they'd cut mine.

Jack Carter worked for Joe for years. I was glad to see him get the shop when he got it in 1950.

Along in the early sixties, after I put in a hard day's work in the shop, my youngest daughter Kathy used to come down to sweep. She and a girlfriend were in high school, and they wanted to earn a little money. It was nice to have the two of 'em down there rather than just one alone. I'd give 'em a key, and they'd go down and scrub it up so the appearance was neat and clean for the weekend and the next week.

I always got a kick out of it because I had a one-pound coffee can full of Tootsie Rolls which we gave the kids in those days. But my Tootsie Rolls would be pretty much gone by the time Tuesday came around. The girls knew where those had gone!

Then in 1972, I got a letter in the mail; my landlord wanted twice the amount of my lease because Dayton-Hudson had offered that much. They were talking about putting in a pants store at that time. Well, that was pretty high rent.

When I gave notice that I wasn't going to take it, the back part of my shop was an L shape. Then, when the landlord came out and took a look at it, he said, "I didn't know that it was like that." Rosemary's Beauty Shop next door had more space than I did. But it was too late then.

That was when I came over here with Jack Carter. Jack was having the same problem I had; he couldn't get a new lease at 5012 France, so he came over here to this location in 1972.

When I came across the street here, I rented my chair.* So I brought all my customers with me. I don't know of any of 'em who didn't come. I was fifty-eight years old, and I wanted to keep building up my social security until I was sixty-five. It worked out real good for me.

*When a barber rents a chair from the owner, a percentage of each haircut goes to the shop.

Vern cutting Dale Messer's hair in 1972.

George Hartzell, ca. 1950.

Fred Willson, 1954.

George Willson, ca. 1930.

Personalities

Joe Danens, 1953.

C. J. "Sonny" Danens, ca. 1960.

Sid Gunn, 1986

Mabel Millam Willson in the Minnehaha Grange Hall in October 1963, when the hall was celebrating its 90th anniversary. Behind her is a portrait of Mrs. George Baird. As a child, Mabel would polish the oil lamps in the grange hall chandeliers.

The Willsons

Where I lived from 1939, the year I was married, to 1943 was the Willson farmhouse at 5340 Normandale Road. They had more room than they needed, so they rented the second floor to us for ten dollars a month. Originally, it was all bedrooms upstairs, but we utilized it as a kitchen, living room and one bedroom for the two of us and, towards the end there, for my daughters Vernice and Phyllis.

They had an outside stairway to the back door. There was an outhouse, and water had to be carried up and down the stairs. The well was adjacent to the barn. It had a windmill, but you had to pump your own. I had a twelve-quart pail that I carried the water in. Under the sink we had what we called a slop pail for the used water. We had a spout like you have now, only it drained into a pail. You'd open the door underneath there, take the pail out, take it downstairs and throw it in back. When I'd bring the water up for washing clothes, my wife would boil it, and then we would put it in the washing machine.

When we cooked, we had a kerosene range with an oven. We heated the rooms with a kerosene stove that I got on my own, what was called in those days a pot burner.*
It was about three and a half feet high, about thirty inches wide and about twenty-four

*As opposed to a wick burner.

Vern, his wife Wilma, and his daughter Phyllis on the Willson farm in 1942. In the background across Normandale Road is the thirteenth hole of Edina Country Club golf course.

George Millam stands by the Edina Mill in 1925. The mill was demolished in 1932, and Millam died in 1935.

inches deep. Heat came out of the hood on the top that had a grill like metal ribbons. It had cast iron legs and insides, and a jacket, a casing that was a medium brown metal with porcelain to give it a nice look. You could adjust it from one to ten according to what the temperature was outside. The only problem was, sometimes you would get too much kerosene right where it came out of the hole into the pot. It would charcoal up like a dark black hard soot. Then you'd have to turn up the burner to burn that off. And sometimes you'd have to disconnect it and run a coat hanger through to clear out the hole.

We had a teakettle on top of the stove so that it would give off steam because that was the only humidifier we had. And then in the morning we had hot water to make coffee and wash and shave. We had a fifty-five-gallon oil drum in the garage that the delivery truck would fill with kerosene every week or ten days in the winter time.

The garden started about a block south of what is now Our Lady of Grace school and went back west from there. From the barn down to Eden Avenue was the cow pasture. I remember seeing it as a pasture because the cows would be in that mud down there up to their ankles. But now it's been filled in, of course.

Fred and Mabel Willson were very wonderful people — nobody nicer or more cordial than what they were. Mrs. Willson's father was George Millam who owned the

Edina Mill and lived right on the golf course. Just south of 50th on Wooddale were two houses, and his was one of 'em. That was where Mabel grew up. They tore down those houses when they built the new culbhouse in the early sixties. The old clubhouse used to be right on 50th. And the mill wheel in Tupa Park now is the one that George Millam used.

Fred had a brother George who lived just a block south of him and was on the Village Council. They had a truck farm together—twenty acres.

I'll never forget one morning. Fred came out of the house to go to the barn to milk the cows, but the Holstein bull got out and met him in the yard between the barn and the house. He wouldn't let Fred out there—just chased him back in the house again. So he called his brother George who came down with his car and chased the bull back in the barn. That same day they called and had the bull loaded and shipped over to South St. Paul—right now. I had always looked at that bull beforehand and thought, "That's a huge animal." So I was quite impressed that day because he weighted exactly 2000 pounds. He was a big one!

The Blacksmiths

In 1936, St Charles' Kitchens was Charlie Lindquist's blacksmith shop. Charlie was not the first blacksmith in that location. His predecessors were John Lilja, who moved the shop to this location from around the corner on 50th Street, and Mr. Moe, who still used to shoe horses and repair ploughshares. Charlie Lindquist stayed in his job until around 1938 when he was around sixty years old. Three years after he left, the concrete-block building was finished off with a brick exterior and became Ruff Furs, Inc. It was several other stores also before St. Charles' Kitchens moved in.

Charlie Lindquist stood about 5' 8" and weighed about 175 pounds In his mouth there was always an inch-long cigar with a matchstick in the end of it. The matchstick was in his teeth so he could use the last of the cigar without burning his lips. He would carry the same cigar around for an hour, and half the time it wouldn't even be lit. He'd try to light it a little more and get a few puffs out of it, and then he'd go on working.

Then some people lived out here on farms who would come in with their tools. But as far as I could see, Charlie's main work in the thirties was sharpening drills for Hemple, a Minneapolis well driller. These drills were flat, four or five inches in diameter, and concaved on two sides for a cutting edge. He heated them in the forge until they were red hot. Then he would lay them on the anvil and hold a cutting tool like a hatchet. But someone had to swing a ten-pound maul. Charlie would come across the street, pound on my window and beckon with his fingers for me to come and swing the maul for him.

I'd go over there pretty near every day. I'd have the maul up in the air, and he'd be moving the cutter. I wouldn't know exactly where the cutter was, but on the way down it would be there, and I would hit it. Then he would take a file to file the drill. When it was a certain color, into the water it went.

There was no conversation. I'd work the maul for about three minutes — maybe fifty strokes, and I worked up a good sweat. I never did get paid for it — that was just exercise. But since I had spent a lot of time on a truck farm from the time I was 15, swinging the maul didn't bother me.

Now Charlie used to drink a lot. Creimen's Restaurant and Beer Parlor was across the street from the blacksmith's, next door to my shop. Creimen and his wife, who lived upstairs, were the owners. When Charlie would go over to get a glass of beer, Mrs. Creimen would have to sell it to him but she'd bawl him out for his drinking. He kept a home brew also in his shop, but nobody ever knew where it came from because it was illegal. He called a gallon of it a "pony" so that nobody would catch on to it. Then he had a telephone number that he would call and tell 'em he wanted a "pony." And he had a sense of humor. Once in a while he would call these people up and say, "I'm awfully busy today . . . you'd better bring me two ponies."

The jugs he buried in the sand of his shop, in the basement under the wooden floor. I bet if you dug down in the sand today, you could still find some.*

Then he got tired of stray dogs around his shop, so he fastened a metal plate to the telephone pole and wired it with electricity. It wasn't long before he scared the dogs away!

Charlie sold out to a fellow by the name of Emil. I always remembered him because I got quite a kick out of watching him pounding on something with a hammer while he was smoking his pipe. One time, he swung the hammer up past his pipe. and the pipe flew all the way across the shop. And I always got quite a kick out of that.

I helped Emil some, too. When he needed somebody to hold something, I went over to help. And I was available. If I wasn't workin', I would go over. He'd beckon for me, and I'd go over and help.

Emil was there probably just two years, and then they closed the shop up and finished the building frame off.

*The basement now has a cement floor.

Sorenson

There was a fella named Sorenson who used to hang around the blacksmith shop every day. When the shop would close up at the end of the day, he would go over and lean against a telephone pole along the sidewalk in front of Fannie Farmer's waiting for time to pass. One day I noticed that the pole was set at an angle from all his leaning on it!

Sorenson was a man about sixty years old. He lived out in the country and at one time milked a few cows — that was his bread and butter. He used to come over and get a shave, and I always had to get quite a kick out of it. He had such a big stomach that when he'd lie in the chair, I used to think, "Boy, that would make a good ski slide!"

George Payne

On the north side of 49th, a black man named George Payne had a hog farm of six or more acres and a garbage dump. There was a house and a barn.* The neighbors in the row of houses there along the west side of France objected to this. If you've ever gone by a hog farm, you know what they're like.

In 1936, Payne was probably in his sixties. He was a short, little guy, easy to talk to. He liked to visit. He used to come for a haircut, but after the shop was closed. He was busy in the daytime — that was just the way he wanted it.

His son drove the garbage truck, a tilt box.** In those days, it was not a dump truck as we have today, but a triple box — a pick-up truck with staples in it, you know. You put two-by-four stakes in and boards around it in sections. With boards on two sides, you have a double box. Then put boards on the end, and it'd be a triple box. That's what they had.

They had a different route every day. They would just pick the garbage up and throw it in the way it was. There wasn't no compacting. For dumping, he'd pull the end gate off the back.

Kent

A fella by the name of Kent used to stop in the barbershop to thaw out. He grew a full white beard and white hair, and he had eyes that looked in all different directions. He was a sorrowful sight — just like something that walked down the railroad tracks — a hobo.

He didn't work, and he lived in a milk chassis that was sitting on the ground by Minnehaha Creek, just off France Avenue. Years ago, they used to deliver milk with horses. They had a milk wagon that set on coils, and they pulled it, you know. And the top of the milk wagon, that had sliding doors to close it, was sitting in this vacant lot, and Kent made his home in it.

---

*Bill Jordan remembers playing in this house in the forties when it was deserted.

**Grace Hansen remembers that when one of the Payne boys was born, George asked the attending physician, who lived in the Country Club area, "Would you feel insulted if we named him after you?" The physician was said to be honored by this.

He slept there. He went in there and would just burn an open fire of chips and newspapers to try and keep warm. He told me, "I use newspapers for sheets because that way I have a clean bed every night."

Then it would get pretty doggone cold when he was livin' in there, and he would come into the barbershop and sit on the radiator until he'd start to thaw out. Well, the smoke on his clothes and his body odor would cause such a stench it'd make you sick. But he had a sister here in town, and once in a while when it got too cold, he went down there.

But he'd come in the shop and sit down, and he always had stories to tell. One time he was talkin' kinda foolish, and he said he was gonna have a fight with the painter on the corner, and was gonna put up a boxing ring on the floor of the shop and charge admission!

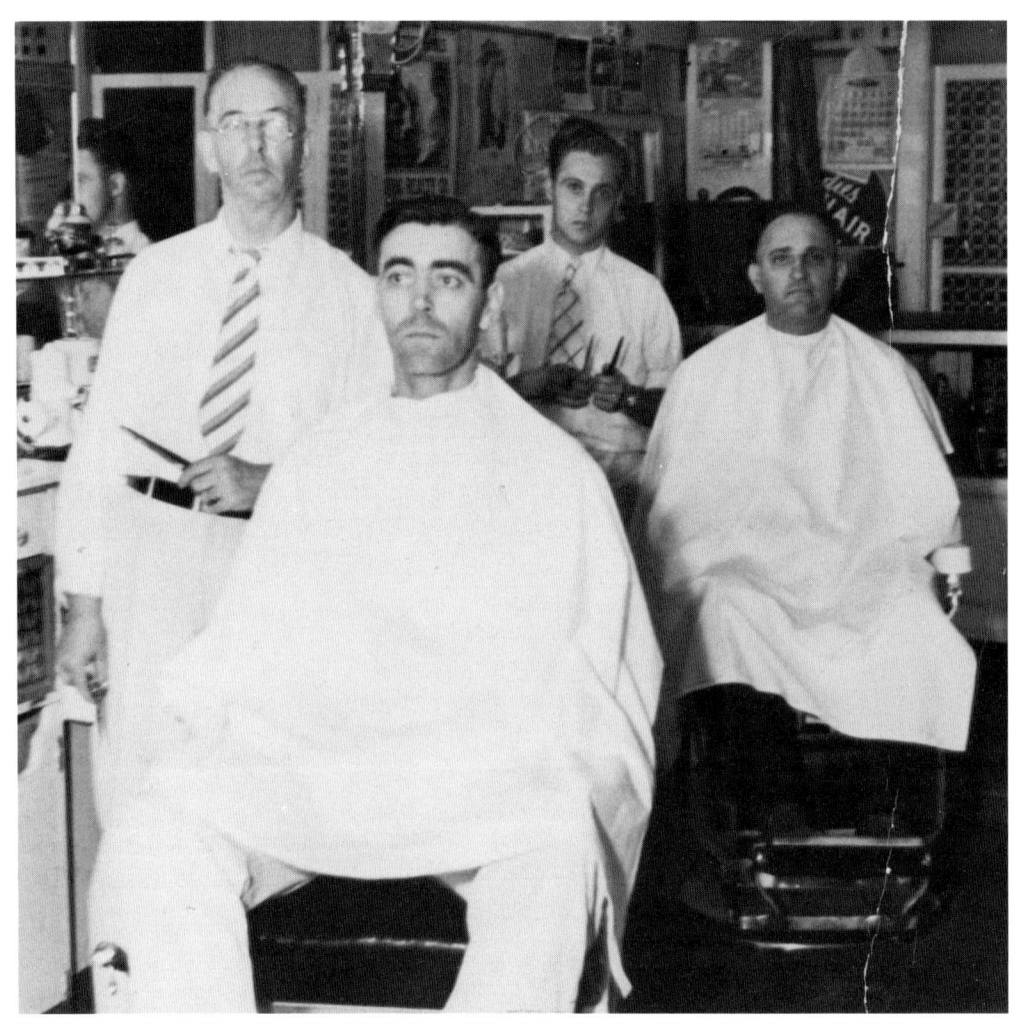

Ed Forberg in 1938 in Bert Davis' chair and Emil the blacksmith in Vern's chair. This was taken by Tisdale, a customer whose hobby was taking pictures and developing them in his basement. He stood in the shop window to take this picture.

Lamitz

There was a man named Lamitz who had been successful in construction work, building houses on Lowry Hill. But by the 1930s he had become a recluse. With hair down to his shoulders, he lived in a tarpaper shack at 56th and France with another fellow in shabby clothes known as Little Joe.

Vern first encountered Lamitz in 1936 when he was in the barber college down on Hennepin Avenue. Lamitz used to come to the barber school for a shave. One day Vern, who was twenty-one, and two other young barbers decided they were going to cut his hair. Lamitz hollered so much that they were unsuccessful. After that, Lamitz never came back to the barber college for his shaves. And when he found out that Vern had moved into "his" neighborhood, he made a wide berth around his shop at 50th and France.

One day in the early forties, Lamitz was drunk as a skunk. He come home early one morning. He had little Joe with him. They must have been in a bar all night because here Joe was, trying to help Lamitz along, y'know. And he got tired, of course, of carrying him so when he got to the corner up there by the Rexall drugstore, he lifted Lamitz and hung him over the mailbox so he could rest. That was when T. E. Tilly, the policeman, came along in the squad car and he seen this here, and Little Joe seen the squad car and got scared. So he just dropped Lamitz on the sidewalk and ran all the way home. But Tilly got out of the squad car, went over and picked Lamitz up. He loaded him in the car and took him home.

Another time Lamitz seen something funny near where he lived, and he wrote a poem about it. A fella was haulin' a load of hay along Minnehaha Creek there near France Avenue. "That was a trick/ridin' down the crick," I think Lamitz wrote. The team of horses was going parallel to the creek, but it got top-heavy as it was going on the slant. All the hay with the fella on top of it dumped into the creek. The horses were still movin' and he was ridin' down the creek on the hay. I imagine he got pretty wet before he got outta there. I found out about it because Sonny Danens recited the poem to me.

The Ice Cream Man

In 1936, Ed Forberg had been operating his Country Club Ice Cream store for about five years. His building was on the west side of France, south of and adjacent to Nolan's. Forberg used to park his delivery truck in a driveway between his store and the blacksmith shop.

What Forberg made his money on was meringue pies, about twelve inches round, that he would make and decorate and take out to parties. Some of these monied people out here would have a birthday party for their kids or a party for their company at night, and they would order one of these. And in order to take a truck to deliver them, he had to get pretty good money.

When he made that ice cream, it was like ice cream that was melted. Then he'd mix it and put in on the shelves of his walk-in freezer. The dry ice would freeze it.

Then he also had a soda fountain there, and a lot of people bought cones. His ice cream was richer and more expensive than other ice cream because it was made out of *pure* cream. But it was hard to hold a cone. You'd buy an ice cream cone, and it would run down your sleeves in a matter of seconds. So it was 100% — there was no gelatin, like other companies used.

He had almost as many flavors as we got now. I liked pistachio nut — I still do. In those days, those shells that he made for the ice cream pies would have been too much for my budget. I just ate the cones.

Ed come to me one day and said, "You know, I did a very foolish thing today."

"What was that?"

"I bought a piece of property. Paid $1500 for it!"

He built on it and operated his ice cream business here for quite a few years. This building was later the first location of the Americana State Bank and now is the Kreiser Real Estate building. But when Ed paid $1500 for that lot, he really thought he got took. Think of what it would be worth today!

Big Gus and Little Gus

There was two plumbers on this corner, and the both of 'em was Gus. In back of my barbershop was a vacant room, and Big Gus Hoaglund put his pipes there and stored 'em. He had a space in there of about 24' x 30' that he stored his pipes in, and there was an entry way from the alley. When he sat down in the chair to get a shave, why his stomach was just like a toboggan slide. So that was Big Gus.

Little Gus Hegstrom was the plumber that 'most everybody on the corner used. At one time, he worked for Big Gus, but when Little Gus went on his own, Big Gus took on more contracting jobs. Big Gus was more installing new stuff. But if I had sewer problems in my house, who'd I call? I'd call Little Gus. He worked out of his house at 47th and France. He was a hard worker, and he knew what he was talkin' about.

He was a little Swede and strong as a bull. He was always in the barbershop here, and in and out. Every time he'd come in, why he'd lingo off a vocabulary of Swedish. I didn't understand what he was talkin' about — he did. But he always got a lingo goin', and I would get a kick out of it. And he had a lot of sayings, you know, just like we have in English. He sure could talk! He must a' talked *all* the time at home as a kid!

So, there was Big Gus and Little Gus.

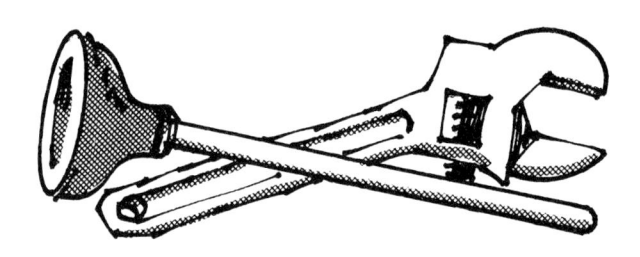

Fred Gaulke (Gohlke)

In back of Krieser's building, a cement man named Fred Gaulke had probably an acre, maybe a little more. He was a bachelor for many years, and then he married Mrs. Moe, whose house was right back there by 51st and Halifax, just about where the curve is. But, you see, Halifax didn't come through—that was a dead end. There was no road at 51st there either—only Fred's driveway. All around his bungalow was a row of Lombardi poplars, and the driveway went between the trees.

  Fred raised raspberries there, kind of as a hobby. I don't know as he ever grew enough of them to sell to the grocery store, but he sold to people that ordered them. Word of mouth.

  He was a plasterer. He contracted out. I had him put in a ceiling, and he made four or five trips down to my house. He drove a black Model-T Ford truck with a big bed in the back. You know, I always got a kick out of those trucks. If you loaded the back too heavy, you could take the crank and lift the front end of it up. You could hardly steer it because the front wheels would be off the ground! It had what we would call bang boards on the back. I used to call them bang boards because when we picked corn, they were boards that had two slats on each end, and they would fit down over the ones that was there. We called them bang boards. But he had his equipment in there.

  Poor old guy, he got weaker and weaker along in the early sixties. His heart was so bad that I'd see him—he'd carry a stool along with him when he'd come up to the corner. He would get out on France Avenue, and he'd put down his stool and sit down for a bit. And then he'd get up as far as the Kreiser Building, and he'd sit down again. He died not long after that.

Little Erick

We used to have a carpenter on the corner named Erick Bjorkmann, and we called him Little Erick. He worked out of his home on 49th Street, and he worked alone. He was a good carpenter, but he had palsy of some kind. I used to watch him. His head was shakin' and his hands were shakin'. His hammer would be up in the air, and the nail would be goin' back and forth. But when he came down on it, he went right for the head.

  He built several buildings on the corner. One was Nolan's new building over where Twin City Federal is now, and it was a nice looking building. After Twin City Federal decided to put up a new building, I always thought, "Gee, it's a shame to tear that down!"

Home Haircuts

  In the 1930s and 1940s, it was a practice to make house calls quite freqently for haircuts and shaves when a customer was hospitalized or homebound because of illness. Vern would leave his shop to do this for forty-five minutes or so when it wasn't busy.

C. J. Hoigaard, ca. 1948.

Nils Benson, ca. 1948.

I used to go out and cut Jack McNellis' hair and shave him when he was laid up in bed. I charged him just the regular fifty-cent haircut fee. But I felt obligated because they were nice people that patronized me when they were able to be out there.

Then I cut C. J. Hoigaard's hair at home for a while when he broke his hip. Of course, in those days, they had no pin operation for hips. In the thirties, he was sixty-five or seventy years old. I bought awnings from him too over the years for my shop, but by this time his son had already taken over the business. Hoigaard lived on France along the Payne farm. He was well heeled, but a grad old gentleman.

Another one was Nils Benson of Benson Optical. In the thirties, he was in his sixties and he lived at 66th and Vernon. I cut his hair at Methodist Hospital, and then he got so he could come into the barbershop again. But later he had an accident where his car brakes released on his sloping driveway, and his car door pinned him. So he was laid up for another spell, and I used to cut his hair at home and at the Heritage House.

Benson wrote a book, and he gave me one, but I haven't been able to find it. He translated it from Swedish to English. I've wanted to find that so bad!*

Benson was one of the grandest old men that I think I ever knew. He sold his business to Anderson, and he was another one that I cut at home. They were good, Christian men, and I had a lot of deep respect for them. They were grand. Grand people. When I'd cut Benson's hair in the house, I'd say, "I'm here to cut your hair."

"Fine. Do it in the name of the Lord," he'd say.

Then, for a while I cut J. J. Duggan's hair. He was on the Village Council at one time, and he had a farm on the north side of 70th Street, just west of Normandale Road. They've named that Duggan Plaza after him.

After he had a heart attack, I went to cut his hair out there were he lived. This one day, he had gotten out of bed and was sitting in a chair in his bedroom. I cut his hair. He got back in bed and was sittin' there propped up on pillows, and I told him good-bye. His wife was out working in the garden. I left him and went home, but I hadn't any more than got home before his wife called my next-door neighbor, who was their daughter-in-law, and said that he was dead.

I hopped in the car, and I took my neighbor and we went right back out there. It startled me. When I got back, he was sittin' there propped up in his bed in the same position he was in when I left.

*Nils Peter Benson translated Nils Dahlberg's *Under High Command* in 1959. It was the biography of Prince Oscar Bernadotte, a lay preacher and evangelist.

Two Priests

Rev. Leo Gleason, pastor 1935–1941.

Father Gleason was the pastor of St. Patrick's Church in Cahill (Settlement). He was a big man, fairly stout with a growth on his neck in back of his ear. In 1936 he was about sixty-five years old.

He didn't drive a car, so he'd hitch a ride up to 50th and France for a haircut. When he was done, he would wait at Forberg's Ice Cream store for someone who was going that way. One idiosyncracy he had was that he always brought his own comb for the barber to use.

After he left St. Patrick's around 1941, there was another priest, Father Ryan, that took his place during the forties. He was a short fellow, very courteous. He was probably the same age when I was cutting his hair as Father Gleason was. I kinda think that they came over from the bigger parishes to a smaller church like that as they got older.

Rev. George Ryan, pastor 1941–1944.

After I cut his hair, why he would always say, "I want some of that Lucky Strike or whatever-you-call-it." He wanted Lucky Tiger, a tonic. 'Course, Lucky Strike was a cigarette, but he would ask for it that way every time.

Father Ryan's head was as bald as a refrigerator. But he liked the head rub, so we would do that. He was a grand old gentleman.

The Bucketts and Trisler

In 1936, at the intersection of 54th and France, the east corners were vacant lots, the southwest corner was a tarpapered residence, and the northwest corner was occupied by Ernie Buckett's dairy and grocery store, which faced France Avenue.

Earlier, Ernie had built his building for a Texaco station, and his son Earl had run this for a good many years. But they got into a wrangle with Texaco and replaced them with the dairy and grocery store.

This store was operated in later times by a fireman named Chuck. In the fifties Chuck got into an argument with Ernie and built a new building for the dairy store across 54th Street to the west of the tarpapered house.[1]

In the meantime, Earl had built two buildings on the side of the old Texaco station: a hardware store, which he ran, and a restaurant run for a while by a lady named Pfeiffer. Later on, Earl sold the hardware business to a Mr. Miller who, in turn, sold it to a Mr. Smith. Eventually, Smith moved the business to the 50th and France corner.[2]

Smith handled refrigerators and window air conditioners in his hardware store. One time the air conditioning company offered a prize of a Hawaii vacation for two people to the store that sold the most air conditioners. He turned around and had a drawing where people had a chance on a trip to Hawaii. He won the trip all right, and he turned around and gave it to the customers. But if he hadn't won it, he'd have been outta luck!

There was a man named Trisler who owned the vacant lot on the southeast corner. On the lot next to this, he had a grocery store with some meats. When you went to buy something, if you went to buy a pound of bacon, he'd sell you a dozen eggs to go with it. If you bought a loaf of bread, why you had to have a pound of butter to go with it. He'd always ask you what you wanted for your change.[3]

He had eight kids, and they all had to work in the store. Trisler was bald-headed too. So when he come down to get a haircut, he always used to tell me that he was sending one of his kids along to get the rest of his haircut.

Everybody wanted to buy Trisler's vacant lot, but he wouldn't sell. He hung on to it, and when he did sell it in about 1965, he sold the whole shebang. He was in bed not feeling well at that time. When the kids left, it was too much.

Now St. Peter's Lutheran Church next door had been told by the Village of Edina that there wouldn't be an oil station on that corner. But before that, there had been an episode with the property on 66th between Xerxes and France. These older ladies had it, and the Village said it had to go residential, but the owners said it had to go commercial. So they took it to court, and the court let the buildings go commercial. That was why the attorneys for the Village told 'em they didn't have a chance on Trisler's lot. If they took 'im to court, why it'd go the same way. Some people thought it'd be better anyway for an oil station there than a big, high building that would cut the church off so that you'd never have seen it from that side at all.

He sold it then to the oil station — the building that's there now. But the day he got the check, he died of a heart attack. He never got to realize his sale.

1 Now occupied by The Picket Fence, Needlepoint
2 Vern Swanson interview with Sid Gunn, fall of 1986
3 According to Leslie Buckett, much of Trisler's trade was in the Cahill area. (Buckett interview.)

The Painter

There was a painter and decorator around 50th and France that worked out of his house. My boss that I worked for had him, and then one of my customers had him.

The only problem was he drank, y'see. And they'd take him out and get him started on a job, and then he thought he was foolin' people because he carried his hooch next to his coffee in a thermos bottle. Jack McNellis, one of my customers, knew that. So he took him out on the job, and he says to the painter, "Can I have some of your coffee?"

No," he says. "It isn't good for you."

Well," Jack says, "you're drinking it, aren't you?"

"Yeah, but that wouldn't be good for you."

"Anyway," Jack says to me, "I drank half of his 'coffee' because I figured if he drank it all, I wouldn't get any work out of him!"

But, you know, this painter was the type of guy that there wasn't any place hardly he hadn't been. He was always telling me stories about his travels to Florida and Texas and Washington, D.C. So one day I says to Forberg, "Boy, that guy's really been everywhere. And he sounds pretty accurate the way he remembers it right down to the last detail."

"Well," says Forberg, "you know where he gets all that? Down in my basement. He sets down there and reads all them *National Geographic* magazines. He's never been close to those places!"

54th and France on March 1, 1951. Buckett's store is on the right. Bruce Peterson, a nearby resident, is walking the streetcar tracks between "foxholes."

Nelson Brothers

The southeast corner of 50th and France was a Rexall Drugstore in 1936. Around 1927 or 1928, two Nelson brothers had come from Albert Lea to open drug stores in the Twin Cities.* Albert Nelson built on the 50th and France site in 1923. In the next eight years, he had leased the store to his brother Oscar and gotten it back again.

Albert kept uppin' the rent on his brother till it got to the point where he squeezed him out. So he went back in there himself, and Oscar went across the street in one of those buildings on the other side of the Standard Oil Station. He operated there for about a year and a half until it got to a point where he couldn't make it anymore, so he just liquidated.

Then Albert continued on for many years in his location. But at that time it was only a little bit of a thing—maybe twelve feet by forty feet. That's all the bigger it was.

Bert Davis had both Nelsons for customers, and then when he left, I had them for customers. Albert was polite—almost too polite. He used to bow. One time, he wanted a kid to help him after school when he was busy. And I guess the kid didn't have too much to do one day, so he ground up a moth ball in the Alka-Seltzer machine. They had to take it all apart and clean everything, so Albert was just raving. I thought that was the funniest thing. I don't know whatever gave the kid the idea. I used to tease the kid, "Have you ground any more moth balls?"

Nelson owned the property all the way down to the alley, but there was only the drugstore and the Red and White grocery building, and all the rest of it was vacant lot. Then in 1938 he leased the land to a man by the name of Brown, who put his own building up on 50th right next to the alley. This was Sonny's Hamburgers, and later the White Grill, a hamburger shop.

Later on, the White Grill was sold to a man by the name of Frank Young, and he ran it for a quite a few years until about the time they ended the war. About this time, Nelson, who only owned the land, wanted to squeeze Young out, and he gave 'im notice to move. Then Young sold the building to Bill Olson. You know, that was kind of a funny deal, in a way, because I think Nelson figured that Olson would leave the building there. But Olson had other ideas. He moved the building over to 66th and Penn for a relative to run, and it was over there for quite a few years. Eventually they moved it again—where they moved it to, I don't know.

John

There was an old man at Thompson Lumber named John. He was the manager of the yard out in the back of the building, and he was in his seventies. He used to saw the pieces of wood that the customers needed.

Well, one winter—I suppose it was 1940 or 1941—it was particularly cold. And you know, there are three cold places in the winter: a cemetery, a Christmas tree lot, and

---

*These Nelsons were not related to Del Nelson, the current pharmacist and owner of the buildings, or to the Nelsons who operated a dry goods store on the northwest corner.

a lumber yard—the wood retains the cold. There was no heat from the building back where he was working, and he was wearing gloves. Something from the saw caught in his glove and pulled his finger into the saw and cut the finger off.

Several of those lumber guys were customers of mine. John wasn't, because he didn't have enough hair to cut, but I cut his son's hair a lot. Then one day I was down at the lumber yard and saw him with his hand wrapped up.

"What happened to you?" I says.

"I lost my finger," he tells me.

"You mean after all these years of being careful?"

"Yes, and I would have kept it then if I hadn't been wearing those gloves!"

Haeg

On 58th and Wooddale, on the west side, was a pasture. I took my daughters out there in the forties and I says, "Look at this now, because when you get to be grown up, this is all going to be houses in here." What was there was called the Haeg farm, and it was on the west side of Wooddale from about 58th on out to Valley View Road.*

They were customers of mine. They milked quite a few cows. Haeg was a regular farmer. He had a son, but he lost his wife in the early years, probably in the thirties, and he never remarried. He raised the boy and sold the farm about 1950.

It was kind of a sad deal because one day when the son went to work—he was tending bar—somebody came in and robbed him. Young Haeg was going to defend the place, but he got shot. He died right there, and that was the end of that.

Joe Danens

Joe Danens worked on Dayton's stores and downtown for the courthouse excavating. He did the basement of the sanctuary addition of the Edina Baptist Church around 1973,** and he never charged anything because he was a member of another Baptist church. They named Danens Drive after him.

I'll never forget the day Joe came into the barbershop just raving. He was on the village council, and the council had went and bought a slough hole that was absolutely worthless—no good for anybody. Well, then it ended up that they were going to make Braemar Golf Course out of it.

His son got the contract for filling that hole. He didn't have enough trucks of his own, many as he did have, so he went out and rented some more. They hauled dirt in there in the wintertime after it froze so they could drive a truck on it. They moved a hill! They hauled it in so fast the surveyors couldn't keep up with it and had to go outside and hire surveyors to keep up. So they filled the whole thing with dirt. I often thought, "I'll bet you that with all that moisture underneath, it'll never dry out in the summertime when it gets hot because it'll be fed by moisture underneath." But it made a good golf course.

*Vern remembers Tedman's Grocery Story across the street from the Haeg house, on the southeast corner of Valley view Road and Wooddale.
**Now Grace Church

Places and Events

50th and France around 1944. 50th Street runs diagonally west to the bottom right.

Elgin Creamery

Before I came here, and before the Edina Theatre was built in 1934, all this area between the theatre and the bowling alley belonged to Elgin Creamery. Delivery was done with horses, and the Edina Barber shop is where some of the barns for the creamery were. They would bring their loading and stuff down here.

Then there was a hole that was real low, right close to where the driveway was later for the theatre parking lot. They dumped glass in the hole — empty bottles, broken bottles. So then when the theatre came in there they filled all that in with dirt.

But when the Red Barn* came to be built in about 1968 over the old driveway, they made new driveways to coincide with the building. Well, they dug down for the driveway and ran into all this glass, and nobody seemed to know where it came from. I knew where it came from. And there's still a lot of glass under there.

Edina Theatre

The Edina Theatre** was built in 1934. Its manager at that time, John Hurley, still comes here for a haircut. They wanted to build this here theatre on 50th and Xerxes, but the neighbors there got up a petition to keep 'em out because of the parking. They didn't have the parking space, and the residents didn't want the parking around their homes.

Here they can park many, many cars. You used to enter the parking lot from France Avenue where Arby's is. There was a parking lot attendant, Walt Oxborough, who was a retired man living across the street from the theater, and he was always there with his flashlight helping people park. The lot went from the theatre to the bowling alley and from France Avenue to about twenty feet beyond the theatre. So I often said that the theatre is what made this corner. It drew people from all over for the show.

Then they wanted the businessmen to pay for the theatre parking lot 'cause a lot of people came and parked their cars down there and visited and shopped on the street. I don't think the businessmen particularly contributed, so the theatre used to put a rope across up there to keep people from parking. They just opened it at night.

The parking lot was actually a hole. It was probably four feet below the level of France Avenue. When you came into the parking lot, you came down a ramp, and the rest would be all gravel. There was a cable fence along the edge of the sidewalk to keep people from walking off the edge. The fence was there from when the old Elgin Creamery was on that lot.

Sometimes in the thirties they would have what they called bank night. They stood up on the stage between the shows and called off names for cash prizes — ten or twenty dollars. One time they called George King's name, and he wasn't there. So somebody ran down to the drugstore, and he came running right back to get his money.

---

*In 1988 this is Arby's.
**The spelling was changed from "theatre" to "theater" around 1947. According to John Hurley, the first owners were Benjamin and Israel Freeman.

I also remember when I was in there to a show in the summer, it was so cold that we really enjoyed it, but when we came out—why, it was so hot that the drastic change made me stagger on the sidewalk. And that was the only air conditioning that there was on 50th and France in 1936.

Then in summers I used to come and get water at the theatre's artesian well. At that time, they used the water to air condition the theatre. I was told the well was 850 feet deep, and I remember the water was very, very cold. You see, they had a pipe and a spigot coming out of the wall. Anybody could use it, but nobody used it as much as we did. We would take and go over there from the barbershop with a quart milk bottle, and we would catch water coming out of there because it was ice cold. Boy, that was sure good drinking water!

Edina Theater, shown here in the 1970s, was built in 1934. The first movie was *On the Good Ship Lollipop* with Shirley Temple.

Bowling Alley

> Below all the shops of the Lucille Smith building, there are still the lanes of a 1938 bowling alley.[1] These lanes were built by Sy Ryan and called the Edina Recreation Center. A 1941 ad refers to soundproof alleys and air cooling.[2]

In 1938, that was *the* bowling alley of the Twin Cities. It had eight alleys upstairs and eight downstairs. They had a beer license and a short-order cafe. You could buy a hamburger, and you could buy pies from the Rainbow Cafe—they were supposed to be superb.[3]

One thing was kinda sad, in a way. They put the plumbing in there and they hooked the hot water to the toilets instead of the cold water. And a woman came in and sat down on the toilet and got her seat scalded. So they had a suit on their hands. I just can't imagine!

Sy Ryan, the owner of the bowling alley, is a very nice person. He owned it for several years, and then, in the late forties when the Biltmore Lanes came in on Vernon Avenue, he sold it and went into the hearing aid business. Now he's retired and must be close to eighty.[4]

> Originally, the pins, which were at the west end of the building, were hand set. In order to bring in the large automatic pin setters, a hole had to be made in the wall about where the door of the present Edina Barber Shop is located. These were removed again when the bowling alley closed, but the polished boards were never removed because of the labor cost. This is why a visitor can still see, between office desks and stored boxes, five of the eight lanes still in playable condition. But now, in place of gutters and ball returns, there is plywood, to make a continuous, level floor.

The White Grill

The White Grill was a hamburger shop that looked like the White Castle—it was the same sort of set-up. It was just a small room with no booths, but there was a bar in a kind of a half-horseshoe. They had maybe eight to ten stools around the bar, and they had a footrest that people put their feet on while sittin' on the stools.

Just as you came in and looked straight ahead was the grill where they fried the hamburgers. They had a big pot that they cooked beans in. Then they had a little quarter-pint crockery pot—just a serving—that you paid a nickel or a dime for. It was blue on the outside and white on the inside. They would dish up the beans, pour 'em in there,

---

1 The shops are Lucille Smith Interiors, Camera Center, Logos Bookstore and The Edina Barber Shop.
2 Edina Directory, 1941.
3 There also seems to have been a hobby store in the building, named Miller's Hobby House (1941) and Cook's Hobby House (1942).
4 The bowling alley was remodeled for shops in 1972.

give you a spoon. It was a big cooker they had — it probably held three gallons. Then they would cook up what they needed for the day.

That was a fine restaurant, and it was handy for us. We would get breakfast there on Saturday morning, and we went in there for lunch.

France Avenue

Ray Garrison plows snow on a Country Club street ca. 1938.

At that time, there was a two-way stop sign at France Avenue, with 50th Street being the through street. Fiftieth was paved with concrete, while France was tarred from 44th to 54th. For eleven years, since 1925, the Como-Harriet streetcar had been coming as far south as 50th; before that, it had stopped at 44th. In 1936, there was a turnaround at 50th and 54th Streets, but with the traffic congestion, particularly from the Piggly Wiggly and the Red and White grocery stores, businessmen asked the streetcar company to move their turnarounds to 51st. And so from 1945 the streetcar turned around at both 51st and 54th Streets. Service ended in 1954.*

In the spring of the year, there was big chuckholes in France Avenue — so deep that Cedric Adams in his column one time in the forties called them foxholes. A car would come through and, of course, they didn't know how deep they were because there was just water ahead. Once there was water spashed clear up to my window — that's how deep it was!

I was thinking the other day — talk about rain — I saw it rain so hard once in the early fifties that I walked out and looked up France towards 54th, and I saw whitecaps in the street — it was raining and blowing so hard. I thought to myself at the time, "This is something I'll probably never see again!"

And I can remember when I first came out here, they used to plow the snow from 51st down to 50th with a team of horses. It was a private individual by the name of Ray Garrison, and he just had a regular wooden wedge. That was kind of unusual.

Someone else who had beautiful horses was Danens in the construction business. Danens dug the basement for the White Grill on 50th in 1938 with a team of horses; that was the last basement that I can remember being dug out with horses and a scraper.

There was handles on what we call a scraper. And you had your handles like you would a plow: you'd raise up, and it would bite deeper. You'd push down, and it would come out. I would say the scraper was probably about three foot wide and about the same the other way. And it had like a scoop shovel — just like the baskets they use now. The horses were hooked onto it, and you could hold it up until it was full. Then you would push down, and it would go up. Then they would pull it out and load a truck with it.

*Russell Olson, *Electric Railways of Minnesota* (Hopkins, Minnesota: Minnesota Transportation Museum, 1976), chapter 2.

My brother and I dug a basement one time for a fella. We got ten dollars for digging the basement, and we worked two days on it. I got my fingers pinched between a rock and the handle; then I pushed it out and squeezed it, so I lost the whole nail and got a felon on my finger. So I know what digging basements was all about. We probably could have had fifty dollars for it just as easily as ten, but we were kids — probably fifteen years old.

A construction scraper for excavating basements. Edina, ca. 1925.

Armistice Day Snowstorm

Another thing that happened during those years was the 1940 Armistice Day snowstorm. While I was home for lunch that day, I dug my dahlia bulbs at twelve-thirty, and then I returned to the shop. It was raining first, and then it was turning to snow flakes.

By three o'clock, it was storming so bad I thought I'd better head for home. The wind out there was blowing so hard that I thought I was going to go down the embankment of that hill where Perkins is and roll over! And I was afraid of going off the road because the snow was so blinding, and I couldn't see one thing. So I left the car and walked across Normandale Road to my house, which was where Our Lady of Grace church is now.* I got a shovel, and my wife Wilma came back with me while Mrs. Will-

Excelsior Boulevard between France Avenue and Lake Street after the 1940 Armistice Day blizzard. Vern remembers that when they plowed this street, they found a man who had frozen to death.

*Normandale Road, or Hwy 100, at this time was a tarred, two-lane county road. It was built as a WPA project between 1935 and 1937, and it was called Lilac Lane because of the many lilacs planted along the highway between St. Louis Park and Golden Valley.

son downstairs babysat our six-week-old daughter. But walking back, the wind was so bad it took your breath away. It'd just suck your breath away, and I'd never experienced that.

It took a total of two hours to go those last four blocks. The snow was packed so tight in the driveway that the car sat there for two days before I could get a push and get 'er started again.

The next morning I walked to work, but all day I had only one shave. And we were without streetcars on the corner for three days because the switches were all frozen shut.

Windstorm of 1950

In July of 1950, we had a tornado that passed over us, but the lightning and the wind were so strong that they struck the chimney on the building we were in and knocked it through the roof. It was quite a high chimney, and it just missed a baby that was in its crib when the bricks came through the bedroom.

We had such a terrible downpour that just flooded in, and the water ran down the stairway from the apartments up there. It was coming through the hole where the chimney was, and it came down through the ceiling of the shop too.

I called my brother who lived in Robbinsdale, and when he came out to help me, we worked until midnight mopping up water. Then he went home, and I worked until four o'clock in the morning. That was on a Friday night. I finally got it cleaned up, I put some pans there where it was drippin' the worst, and I went home and slept a couple hours. Then I came back and cleaned some more so I could work on Saturday. That way I wouldn't have to be closed.

That was the same time the tornado went through Richfield and demolished several homes. In this area, the wind was so strong that they were having meetings down there on 42nd and France on the Morningside of the street, and it blew the tent over and injured quite a few people there.

50th and France ca. 1947. 50th Street runs diagonally east towards the bottom left.

WALKING TOURS

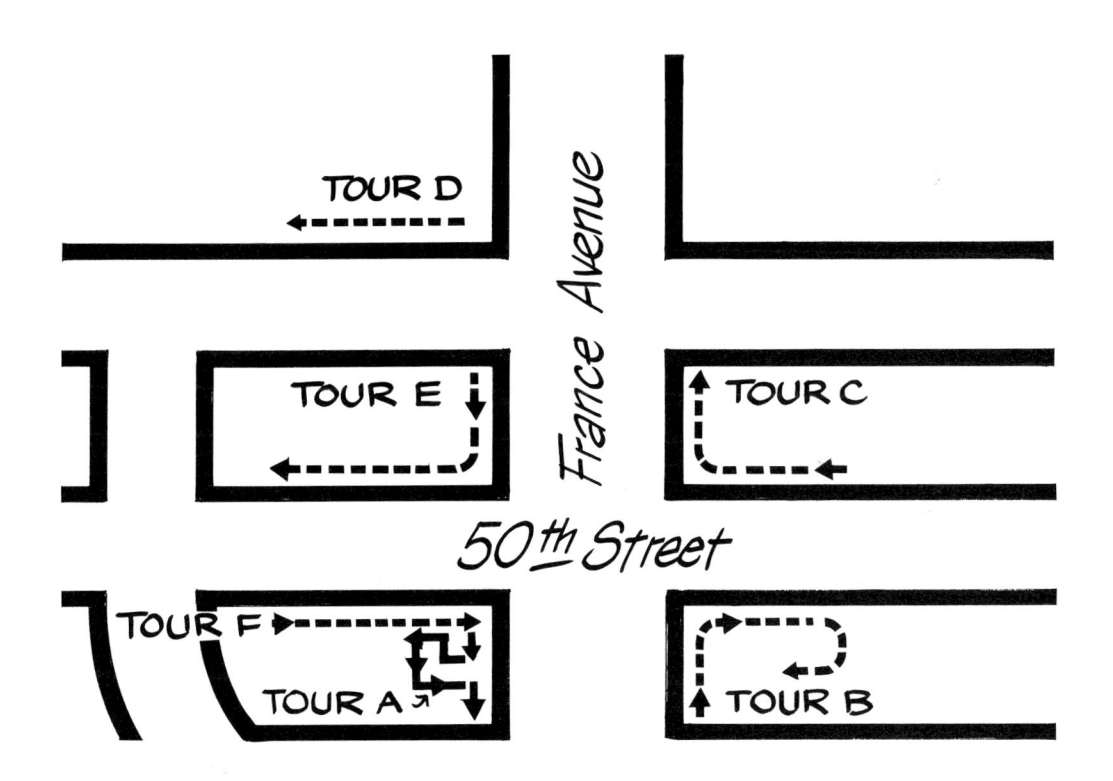

TOUR A:
SW Corner of 50th and France. Walk South

5000 France (Fanny Mac)
5002 France (Korst & Sons)

These first two stores were Nolan's Cafe — a restaurant, beer parlor and bakery all in one. The main door was on the corner. The metal door one step up at the north end of the Korst building was his back door.

There was a bar in the back, here on the south wall. From the front door along the street wall were booths where he served food. On the wall opposite the booths was a showcase that had bread and bakery goods. He had a baker do his baking in the basement. The kitchen was in the back of the bar. It was pretty good food. You got a rounded-out meal: roast beef, potatoes and gravy, vegetable.

In 1941, Nolan built a building up there where Twin City Federal is now, and he locked the doors on this building here and paid the rent so that people would come up there. If he would have done different, why somebody would have opened another beer parlor and restaurant, and people would have walked right in without knowing that he left.[1]

5004 France (Shoe Bop)

Here was Ed Forberg's Ice Cream store. About half way down the store, where that partition wall is now, there was a counter all the way across. He made his ice cream in the basement, and then he had freezers to store it in.[2]

5006 France (Poggios)

This was where Ed Forberg backed in to load up for his deliveries. In 1941, they put this very narrow building here. The first occupant was Egekvist Bakery where they sold baked goods that were brought out from downtown. Then for a while Edina Realty was in here. Michael Davitt started that over on 50th Street. After he left, he sold it to Porter around 1941.[3]

5010 France (St. Charles Kitchens)

This was Charlie Lindquist's blacksmith shop. See page 53.[4]

5014 France (McMuffee's)
5016 France (The Club Room)

The doors here have been changed in recent years. The section farthest to the north (5012) is the site of the barbershop owned by various people, from Joe Barnes to Jack Carter. This shop first opened in 1937 as a radio repair shop, followed the next year by appliance sales in the front half of the building. The doorway was on the south end of the building.[5]

The next two sections were added, first one and then the other, in the forties. The first occupant of 5014 in 1942 was the dental office of Dr. James Madden. There were blinds on the window of the waiting room in front.

This middle section was what they called Knit and Purl. Here's where they got their start. Later they moved across the street, and then later they sold to people by the name of Hill, who operated it until a couple years ago. The Hills sold out to a lady who moved it to her home, but it exists no more.

The last one was a dairy store that started up at Ed Forberg's after he moved out. Then a fella by the name of Merl Fuller built this store. After Merl, the owner was Les Steele. He had milk, butter, and light groceries until he died in 1970. Just to the south of this store was a driveway where they backed in to deliver milk.

*Walk West and then North to the
back of these buildings*

5018 France (Nancy's Nest)

In 1946, this A-frame building was built as an office for the despatcher of the Edina Auto Livery. A fella by the name of Verlin Balfanz started this cab company. They parked the cabs in this parking bay.[6]

On the southeast corner of the Edina Theater there is a concrete platform with a manhole cover. This is the location of the artesian well and the spigot used for drawing drinking water. The spigot has been removed and covered over.

Shapes of these buildings can be distinguished from the back: Nolan's has a flat roof; the Egekvist building is lower; the blacksmith's has a pitched roof, though the front wall in 1936 was high enough so that the roof slopes did not show. The cement blocks, which are the pre-1940s size of 24″ x 6″, can still be seen behind the A-frame building and along the side wall of the 3905 W. 50th building; this was Hartzell's garage. The same blocks are visible behind the blacksmith's shop and Egekvist's bakery.

5022 France (Lucille Smith Building)

In 1938 this whole building, first floor and basement floor, was the Edina Recreation Center, Sy Ryan's bowling alley. The entrance was in the same place.[7]

5036 France (Frank Kreiser Real Estate)

This building was built in 1940 by Ed Forberg as a new home for his Country Club Ice Cream. He had two entrances, one where the current door is and one on the south side. A lot of people used the one on the side quite a bit because it was by the parking lot.

He had a U-shaped counter here right ahead of the front door. You could get a cone or whatever you wanted. You could buy ice cream in bulk. They packed it and weighed it because it had to weigh a certain amount. The scale was right on the counter.

After Forberg went out, he sold the business, and they moved it across the street.

Then the Edina State Bank, later called the Americana State Bank, was in this building for a few years. You can still see the window in the south wall that was the drive-up teller's window.

5050 France (Americana State Bank)

In 1949 this was Hauschild's Insurance, but they had just the main part. When the bank moved in here, they added on the part of the second floor that's over the parking area.[8]

Fifty-first Street did not go west of France in 1936. What was there was a private driveway that led up to Fred Gaulke's house, and this stood about where the Southwest corner of Lund's is.[9]

Ed Forberg (left) and Leo Nolan (right) celebrate their 25th anniversary of business on 50th and France in September 1956.

A Good Place To Shop!

RED & WHITE FOOD STORES

MODERN AS THE HOUSEWIFE OF TODAY

The modern housewife has set the standard for our store—clean, bright and comfortable — a good place to shop!

WHERE YOU GET THE BEST VALUES!

A complete line of Groceries, Fresh Fruits, Fresh Vegetables, and Meats. Properly aged beef —cuts for all special occasions— as well as economical cuts.

FRIENDLY SERVICE
FREQUENT FREE DELIVERY

Charge accounts solicited from responsible people.

Knutson & Turner

50th St. at France   Walnut 6966

MEMBERS OF

THE RED & WHITE STORES

TOUR B:

NE Corner of 51st and France. Walk North.

5057 to 5047 France

This was a vacant lot with a diagonal path starting at 5047 and cutting across to the alley. Just grass here, and people walked the path.

Then Bob Kalland's oil station was here from about 1960 to 1985.

5045 France

This private residence had the same owners in 1936.

5037 France (Southwest Professional Building & Parking Lot)

There were two more residences here like the 5045 residence. They were owned at that time by Milton Christianson who later sold them to Anderson, the electric people. Around 1940, Anderson moved the two houses out and filled in the holes. The lots stood empty for a while before a dentist, Dennis Madden, built the building at 5037 France.

5035 to 5015 France (Vacant Lots in 1936)

In the late fifties, Anderson Electric built the building from 5035, which is Holiday Coiffures, to 5025, which is General Sports. There was a meat market here at one time, and Knit and Purl relocated here, too.

In the early fifties, Anderson built the building from 5015, which is Scruples Boutique, to 5023, which is Skeffington's Men's Formal Wear. Anderson himself was in the first part of it (5015–5019), and Country Club Buffet was in the other part (5021–5023). Country Club Buffet was Ed Forberg's ice cream business along with a restaurant that had stools around the south wall. But it was here only about a year before it went bottom up.

5013 France (Bing Plumbers)
5013½ France (Le Knit de France)

This two-story building was the Creimen Building. Creimen and his wife had a restaurant and beer parlor, and they lived upstairs.

Along the north wall were booths, on the south wall was the bar, and in the back was the kitchen.

Creimen sold the business around '38 or '39 to a fella by the name of Bob. After about two years, he sold out to Carlson. Then a couple years later, the 13th Ward went dry. Carlson couldn't make it without selling beer, so he closed. Then Oscar Bergerson, the plumber, bought the building.[10]

Creimen's restaurant and beer parlor in the late 1930s. Earlier this building was the creamery office from the Edina Theater site.

5011 France (Fashions to Boot)

This was a vacant lot in 1936, a hole down there. They had a railing fence along the sidewalk. Then when Bergerson bought the building next door in 1953, he bought this lot and built this building for Bill Korst, Sr. Then for a number of years this was a donuteria.

5009 France (Fashions to Boot)
5007 France (Apartments)

5009-south was Bert's Barber Shop, and 5009-north was Hilma Erickson's Beauty Shop.[11] I got along very well with the beauty shop owners. Hilma sold out around 1940 to Mary Kiesel who was born and raised on France Avenue. She owned it till about 1965 when she sold it to Rosemary Lavesnich, who kept it until 1973. When I left in 1972, Rosemary moved into my place because it was smaller and cheaper to rent. She continued there until about 1974, when she quit. Upstairs there were five apartments and a dentist, Dr. Wessel.

Edina Drugstore, early 1970s.

5005 France (Fashions to Boot)

This was Perl Lotion. The owner was using his own chemicals and making up a lotion for chapped hands. The windows were all covered over, so there was no walk-in business.

The first occupant, back before I came, was a fella by the name of Winn, who had a hardware store. From what Bert used to tell me, that was the most up-to-date hardware you ever saw. But he was ahead of his time. And then somebody got into him for a lot of money, and he went broke.

Then after Perl Lotion, a dry cleaning establishment came in around 1939, and they were there for a few years.[12] When they went out in 1948, Singer Sewing Machine was in there for about fifteen years until they went out to Southdale.

5001 France (B. Dalton)

Nelson's Rexall drugstore was only about twelve feet wide in 1936 — about to where you see the first shelves of books now. Nelson sold out to George King. He was very kind and would deliver prescriptions to the home, if needed. Then he sold to Barnes.[13] The pharmacy counter in 1936 was on the south wall.[14]

3833 W. 50th St. (B. Dalton)

Knutson and Turner's Red and White Grocery, when it was in this location in 1936, was also very small. Before I came, there was a groceryman here by the name of John Buckett, Ernie's brother. He was the first one to rent from Albert Nelson.

The meat counter was on the east wall. On the west wall was a counter with groceries behind it. When they waited on customers, they took cans from the higher shelves with a pole that had a grappling device. They had deliveries too.

3831 W. 50th St. (Edina Pharmacy)
3829 W. 50th St. (The Raven Gallery)

These were vacant lots in 1936.

3825 W. 50th St. (Raven Gallery)
This is where Sonny's Hamburgers was built in 1938. See page 71.

3821/3811/3801 W. 50th St (Peterson Portraits/Edina TV/Standard American Bldg.)
All this property from the alley to Ewing down half a block or so was Thompson Lumber Yard. They were at this location from 1927 to 1953. I went in there once and bought a Yankee drill—the kind where you push in and back on the handle. I still use it, and it works as good as it did then!

Walk South down the alley a few doors

5005
When Winn's hardware store was here, this driveway went down to the basement. After Boller bought the building, he filled this in around 1944, and I was glad he did because we had rats and mice continually. He'd poison 'em and they'd stink to high heaven. When he filled that in, we didn't have the problem.

5009
This is the door to Gus' Plumbing. He would back his truck up to this platform. This doorway did not go through to the barber or beauty shops. Then when Boller bought the building, he built this garage.

5011
The sign *Le Petit Cafe* is left over from a cafe located here around 1974.

50th and France ca. 1947. France Avenue runs diagonally south towards the bottom right.

The new Market Street (49½th) looking west, ca. 1942. The garage on the left, which belonged to Leo Nolan, was directly behind his cafe. Keller's drug store is visible between the garage and the round Hartzell sign.

TOUR C:
NE Corner of 50th and Ewing: Walk West.

3808 W. 50th (Pearson's)

When I came here in 1936, this was a Piggly Wiggly grocery. Pearson's is in the same building, but they've added to it on the east side.[15]

About 1947, Piggly Wiggly sold out to Red and White from across the street. Then Winston and Newell put a store in there. They put their shelves at an incline so that they were stocking from behind, and the cans rolled down. They were trying that out for a couple years to see how it would work. After that, it was a carpeting and linoleum store, and after that there was a bakery and Hackenmueller's butcher shop where he sold fresh meats, sausages and bologna.

4951 France (Amoco Station)

This is the third Standard Oil station that's been on this corner. In 1936, the building was no more than ten feet square with a place for the tenant to go in and make change and keep warm. On the outside, to the east of the building, there was the grease pit. This was a hole in the ground, and customers would drive over the top and have their oil changed. There were little steps that the mechanic could walk down. The operator when I first came was Bud Bolduk. One time around 1937 or 1938, the police set up a radar trap in his oil station to catch speeders. But his customers got caught and it hurt his business, so he said, "Hey! Can't you fellows move this further down the street?" So they did.

France Avenue looking south, ca. 1942. Hartzell's used car lot, the Karmelkorn building, and the Gambles store are on the left. The signs for Hartzell Motors and the Village Inn are on the right.

4941 France (Club Tan/Positive Body Dynamics/Alternatives for Nails & Hair)

In the southwest corner of this parking lot, there were two buildings next to each other in 1936. I don't remember the 1936 proprietor of the building to the south, but around 1941 there was a Gambles store there for a year or two that was owned by an individual. Later on it was Karagheusians.[16]

The building to the north was a Karmelkorn shop and a restaurant.[17] After they went out around 1944, there was a beauty operator who went by the name of Kelly. He was a barber, as I understood, before he became a beauty operator. We used to cut each other's hair. He rented this spot for about fifteen years.

Just north of the Karmelkorn building was a lot where Hartzell used to park his cars.[18]

4933 France (Bachman's/Leann Chin)

This is the second Bachman building on this spot.[19]

Bachmans built this building at 4933 France Avenue in 1947. The present building was built after the tornado of 1981.

TOUR D:

NW Corner of 49½th and France: Walk West.

4916 France (Mobil Station)

In 1936, the residences on the west side of France came as far as this oil station property. Jay Kallestad's dad's house was sitting up on a four-or five-foot bank here.[20] The White Oaks Apartments there at 3901 49th St. was just a hole—a wooded area. There was no 49½ St. until around 1948. There was just a driveway between Kallestad's and Jordan's, going around to the back of Hartzell's garage. North and west of this spot was George Payne's hog farm. (See page 55.)

3918 49½ (Patio Village)

The first building on 49½ St. was the Edina Post Office, which went up around 1952. It was the east half of this building. Before this time, the closest full-service post office was at 43rd and Upton. But there was a small branch post office for awhile in King's Drug Store and later in Hartzel's office.

Just to the north and west of this building for awhile in the fifties there was a small hamburger diner set on concrete blocks. It had no basement—they could jack it up and haul it away. It wasn't a very good spot, and it didn't last more than a year.

France Avenue ca. 1945. The Village Inn and Martin Jordan's house are on the left, and Abdiel Kallestad's house is on the right. Kallestad's vacant lot between these two houses had to be sold around 1948 for $2500 so that Market (49½th) Street could be built. Kallestad's house was demolished about 1960.

1924 This residence on the northwest corner of 50th and France was built in 1872. At first it was Trinity Chapel of the Episcopal Church, but it was converted to a residence in the 1880s. This picture was taken from across 50th Street one year before the house was moved to make way for the Gregg Pharmacy building.

1926 The same residence is shown about two years later, shortly after it was moved to its present site.

1975 At present this residence is The Sheridans Interiors on 49½th and France.

1981 A 1972 church window was revealed by workmen while siding was being replaced.

The new Hartzell garage on France Avenue, ca. 1930. George Hartzell is standing with then—partner George P. Lundblad.

A Como-Harriet streetcar in front of Gregg's pharmacy, ca. 1945. The 50th Street turnaround is in the right foreground.

TOUR E:

SW Corner of 49½ St. and France. Walk South.

4924 France (The Sheridans Interiors)
What I remember of this house is that Martin Jordan and his family lived there in the forties.

> The building was built as Trinity Chapel in 1872, converted to a residence in the 1880s, and purchased by Samuel Thorpe and moved to its present site in 1925. Around this time, a half story was added.[21] The last renters before it was put to commercial use were Martin Jordan and his family, who lived there from 1941 to 1948. Martin's son Bill remembers that a printing shop went into the basement in 1948 and that the office of attorney Hosmer Brown, a customer of Vern's since those days, was in what used to be his parents' bedroom.[22]

4930 France (Arthur Dickey Architects)
This was what they called the Village Inn, a restaurant and beer parlor. When I came out here, a fellow by the name of George Hanson owned It. He sold out to Sodergin. The next owner was Pete Heckman, who later sold to George Shalson.

I bought a dinner in here just about every noon hour after the White Grill left. There was a good price on the Special every day — somewhere around $1.75 or $2.00. The bar was on the south wall, the booths were on the north wall, and the kitchen was in back.[23]

> When Art Dickey remodeled the building, he left open, as part of a courtyard design, a grassy plot about ten feet wide that in 1936 was behind eight-foot-high boards. In the forties Bill Jordan and his friends, who sometimes put pennies on the streetcar tracks here to see them flattened, used this grassy, weedy area for playing.

4936 France (Peterson's Edina Mall)
This was the Edina Garage, a Chrysler-Plymouth garage owned by George Hartzell. He had new and used cars and repair work until he liquidated around 1965.[24]

Down near Owatonna, Hartzell had a farm where he raised French cattle for beef. So he returned to the farm, but he got gored to death by one of his bulls. But I knew him real well — he was a very nice fella.

4940 France (Glitz)
This set of buildings goes back to 1925. This first store was the Country Club Beauty Shop around 1940.

4942 France (Merrill Lynch Reality/Burnet)
This was a bakery. I didn't get to know most of the bakers on the corner because they worked nights. The only baker I knew was the one that Nolan had because I used to cut his hair. It was an odd thing, too, because he used to tell me he was like an owl that didn't have any feathers. He wore dark glasses in the daytime, but he could go out and drive in the nighttime and see just like a cat.[25]

4944 France (vacant)
This was the Edina Hardware Store. The owner's name was Bellgam. I can always remember him because when you come in there, his greeting was, "How much can I lend you today?" Later on, Bellgam sold out to Hubbard.

Elmer Adolphson waits on a customer in the late 1930s. His market advertised "carefully selected, properly refrigerated meats, handled and delivered under the most sanitary conditions."

4946/4948 France (James Gang/Kalika)
This was Carl Olson's Grocery and Produce, and, in the same store (4946) Elmer Adolfson's Meat Market. In 1940 the owner wanted more for the rent than they could afford, so both Olson and Adolfson went into Nolan's new building, on the east side of it. Then the Zipoy brothers came in here.[26]

Mrs. Nelson and Betty Gustafson in Nelson's Dry Goods store ca. 1972. Mrs. Gustafson has continued her line of doll clothes in Farmington, Minnesota.

4950 France (Olivers)

This was Henry Nelson's Dry Goods store in 1936. He came along about 1930. I bought a lot of stuff in here because this was the only dry goods store we had on the corner. I bought silk stockings for my wife. I bought the first nylons that ever came out, from Nelson. Fifty cents a pair. And they were great because they didn't run like silk stockings. That was 1940 or 1941.

4952 France (Marty's)

For probably more than 50 years, this was a shoe repair shop. There was a shoe man here when I came. And then Harvey Graff bought the business in 1946 and was here until 1985. His son Jeff has the same business now in Peterson's Edina Mall.[27]

Carl Olson (second from right), Bob Cody (far left), and two others pose behind a counter of his grocery store. Olson's 1935 ad describes a "large line of fresh, staple and fancy groceries."

France Avenue at 46th Street looking north in August 1952. In defiance of the city of Minneapolis and the Twin City Rapid Transit Company, Edina workmen are tearing up the streetcar tracks in order to repave the street damaged by "foxholes."

4954 France (Chico's)
3902 W. 50th St. (Apartments/Doctors' Offices)

This was Gregg's Drug Store in 1936. The building was owned together by Henry "Doc" Gregg, the pharmacist, and Dr. Reuben Erickson. The fountain was on the south wall, to your left as you came in the door.[28] When this moved out around 1967, Marty Donnelly moved here from next door.[29]

3904 W. 50th St. (Shades of Vail)

In 1936, this was Archie Peterson's Barber Shop. (See page 46.) When Marty moved the barbershop next door, Marty's wife opened a drapery shop here. It was here until 1986.

3908 W. 50th St. (Belleson's)

This was vacant land in 1936. At that time, Wes Belleson's dad, Lars, owned and operated a grocery store on 44th and France where Country Club Market is now. Eventually, he sold out to them. But in the forties he was holding it until young Belleson came back from the army. But when Wes got back, he didn't want it. It ended up that he wanted to start a men's store, and this was it.

Doc Gregg, pictured in front of his pharmacy ca. 1950, began has business here in 1929.

3910 W. 50th St. (Vacant)
3916 W. 50th St. (J. Michael Building)

There was a hill here with two houses on top. The first one going west was owned by Billy Kell, who worked for Honeywell. The second was owned by John Oxborough. When Lund decided to build this building in 1946, he had the houses moved two blocks south where they still stand at 5132 and 5136 Gorgas.[30]

The store on the east side (3914) became Town and Country Hardware, and Smith moved down here from 54th and France.[31] The last tenant told me in the seventies when he closed, that the lease came up and he told the landlord, "I wouldn't even pay again the money that I'm paying now, let alone pay an increase."

When this went out, there was a dime store for a while.

3922 W. 50th St. (Carillon Building)

This was the Hay and Stenson Liquor Store with a parking lot to the west. It had a nice brick front and pretty good stock. It was sold by sealed bids to Hosmer Brown and Art Dickey who put this building up in about 1974[32]

3924 W. 50th St. (Twin City Federal)

Here was the second location of Nolan's restaurant, beer parlor and bakery.[33] It was bigger and fancier than the other place. There was a bakery showcase on the left side as you walked in—maybe fifteen or eighteen feet long. There were booths again. He finished it off upstairs with an apartment, and he lived up there. And then it had meats and groceries on the west side.[34] (See pages 79 and 96.) After Nolan died, Mrs. Nolan leased the property to the Edina Cafeteria.

3930 W. 50th St. (Albrecht's)

This was the 1st Edina State Bank, now 1st Bank Edina. When the bank moved to their present location in 1955, this building was bought by Kruse and Gross, Furriers. Gordy Kruse had worked for several years at Schlampp's.

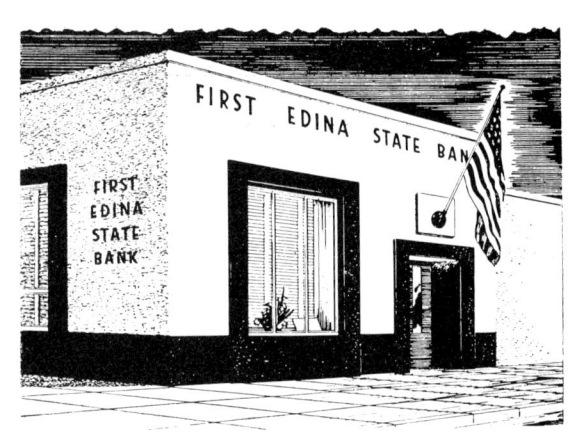

3936 W. 50th St. (St. Louie Bar-B-Que)

Before this building was built, this was Hove's parking lot.

3940 W. 50th St. (Edina 5-0 Mall)

In 1938, Hove's started a grocery store here, and Russ Lund owned the property and ran the meat market. Hove was a friendly old man. He amused me the way he would always stand at the door greeting people. After old man Hove died, Lund wanted to buy Hove's son out for a large sum of money, but he wouldn't take it. Then when Hove's lease ran out, Hove was forced out and went different places. In the meantime, Lund started the grocery business under his own name.

3946 W. 50th St. (James Hager)

This was a clothing shop called Herberger's in 1944. Bert Gamble, who owned the hardware next door, had his first Gamble-Skogmo store in St. Cloud. Herberger also had a clothing shop in St. Cloud as well as in Alexandria, Osakis and Watertown. So Gamble knew Herberger and got him to put a clothing shop in here.[35] Their symbol was a rose. They were here about six years.

3948 W. 50th St. (Clancy's)

Keller Drug Store came here on the first floor in 1946, and at the same time Gamble moved his company store into the basement. Gamble's had a little bit of everything; I remember buying an iron down there.[36]

The space here hasn't changed much from 1940. The doors, the stairs, the pharmacy counter and the fountain are all in the same place.

Across the street where the bank parking lot is, there was a house on a hill in 1936. After World War II, the Edina Library was in this house for a few years. Before that, people would use the library at 43rd and Vincent.[37]

Then on the southwest corner in 1936 was a Texaco station — another one of those pantry-sized buildings.[38]

The Edina Shopping Center and Hoves in March 1947. On the right are Edina State Bank, Olson and Adolphson's, and Nolan's Cafe. National Tea is in the left foreground.

The Wallace residence at 4120 West 50th Street became the first Edina library in 1955. Occupied by the Adams family in the 1930s, it was built in 1872 by James A. Bull.

TOUR F:

SE Corner of France and Halifax. Walk East.

3945 W. 50th St. (Lund's)

In the northwest corner of this Lund's parking lot was the Pure Oil Station starting around 1941.[39]

This whole corner was owned at that time by a man named Fred Sampson who was a wheeler and a dealer. He lived down here to the north of Fred Gaulke at 5017 Halifax. And then a little farther north into the parking lot he had a shack like they have at the state fair. You could walk up to the window counter on the outside and buy firecrackers.[40] Before the Pure Oil Station there was a root beer stand there near the corner, about the size of a garage. I'd see it as I'd go by there.[41]

When National Tea first came in around 1946, they built a store up against the sidewalk.[42] Around 1973, they tore that building down and built the present Lund's building farther back. Around 1976 Lund's took it over.

Brown Derby menu, 1940s.

Edina Eye Clinic building, with art deco design, was on 50th Street next to National Tea from 1939 to 1977.

3939 W. 50th St. (50th and France Building)
From about 1939, there was a doctors' building here, set back aways with grass around it. It was started by Dr. Reuben Erickson, who then sold it in the early forties to Dr. Harry Jensen, Dr. I. H. Moore and several others. Later, it was called the Edina Eye Clinic.

3933 (Children's General Store) through 3917 W. 50th St. (Vacant)
This was a vacant lot in 1936 except for a house at 3917. It was a story and a half, and it set probably thirty feet back from the street. The occupants were Guss and May Krake.[43]

3915 W. 50th St. (The Cottage Sampler)

Here was the Brown Derby Cafe. I used to eat breakfast here many times on Saturday mornings. They always had good food—short orders and a daily special.

It was owned over the years by different people, but the first owner was Bill Olson—the one that moved the White Grill to 66th and Penn. Bill used to own property also on highways 494 and 100, where he raised German short-haired dogs.[44]

3911 W. 50th St. (Edina Theater)

This theater was built in 1934 by Lannie F. Norris, Sr. on the site of the Elgin Creamery. See pages 17 and 69.[45]

3909 W. 50th St. (West: Storm Picture Frames/East: Tidepool Gallery)

Ed Storm has been in this same shop since 1953. Starting in 1948, his brother, Kenneth Storm, had a sporting goods and hobby store here along with Rustin Thayer.[46]

The other store was Anthonie Frock Shop, a dress store. Not long after I came here, they had a fire. I'll never forget it. I was in my shop, and when I heard the sirens, I ran up here. About the time I got to the store, a full-sized mannikin rolled out the window onto the sidewalk ahead of me, and I thought, "Oh no! Somebody's burned to death!"

Then when the firemen got up on the roof, they chopped a hole in the wrong store—Hoyt's Cafe—and later they had to fix that. Eventually, they chopped a hole in the roof of Anthonie's.[47]

3907 W. 50th St. (The Lotus Vietnamese Restaurant)

This was Hoyt's Cafe, a regular restaurant with a dinner menu. There was a Greek that owned it for awhile. And then in 1947 Hasty-Tasty took it over. The owners had one of these stores down on Hennepin and Lake, too. It was a rounded-out good eating place with booths.[48]

3905 W. 50th St. (House of Forrester)

Starting in about 1940, this was Brauer's 5 & 10¢ Store. It had old-style wooden counters in a long row. And the floors were hardwood. Like a lot of those old floors, they got uneven—wavy.

In the basement was where Danens stored his trucks back in the early forties. You could drive in from the theater parking lot in back. Later on, they filled that in (see pages 14 and 65.)[49] When Brauer sold out around 1960, it lasted as a dime store for only about one-and-a-half years.[50]

The driveway to Danens' basement garage in the late 1930s. The large doorway for Danens' trucks can still be seen in the basement of this building at 3905–3907 West 50th Street. The driveway itself, flanked by cement block walls, was filled in and replaced by an A-frame building in 1946.

3901 W. 50th St. (Korst and Sons)

> The current door at 3901 is midway between the 1930's doors of 3901 and 3903. From 1935, France Avenue Beauty Salon was located at 3903. Later, in the 40s, it was Coronet Beauty and then Edina Beauty Salon until 1976. Mrs. Oscar Youngdahl in 1945 sold the business to Grace Hansen who had five operators in addition to a desk girl. Grace, in turn, sold it to a woman named Blanche in 1950.[51]

Nichols had a beauty shop in here. All you could see looking in was rows of hair dryers.
   Next door here is where Edina Realty was in 1939. All you could see in there was a desk at that time. It hadn't grown yet. It took hold when Emma Rovick took it over. She was a well-respected lady and a go-getter.

> After about two years at two France Avenue locations, Bill Korst moved into 3901 in 1955 with a man named Ingram. Ingram sold cameras from a long counter on the west wall, and Korst sold jewelry from a long counter on the east wall. John Loeffler, who had the camera business next, changed the name to Edina Camera around 1960 and moved across 50th Street about a year later. Korst had all of the 3901 shop from that time until the beauty shop next door moved out in 1976. At this time, Korst expanded his store and remodeled the front of the building, changing the location of the door.[52]

The Edina Art and Book Festival during the first week of June 1967. This is the northeast corner of 50th and France. The Edina Cafeteria, visible at the far left, was leased from Mrs. Nolan after her husband's death.

Notes to the Walking Tour

Unless otherwise indicated, the source of these notes is the Edina telephone directories at the Edina Historical Society. They may be inaccurate by one year because of the lapse in time between a change of proprietors and publication of the directory.

1 This one-story building, which includes 3901 50th Street, replaced John Buckett's and Harley Winn's two-story building around 1930 (Grace Hansen interview, August 2, 1987). The last tenant of the old building was probably a hamburger shop (Gene Delaney interview, August 27, 1987). Leo Nolan, however, occupied only the France Avenue side of the new building.

Fanny Farmer was on the corner (5000 France) from 1942 to 1986. After Nolan was established on 50th St., the occupants of 5002 were Brook-Haven Poultry Shop (1943), Marquee Jewelry (1946), W.R. Bliss Jewelry (1947), Beatty-Zephyr Cleaner (1948) and Christian Science Reading Room (1956).

2 When Forberg moved in 1942, the next tenant was Purity Milk, followed by Cody's Market (1947) and Brush's Shoes (1949).

3 Edina Realty was at this location from 1943 to 1953. They were followed by Edina Cards and Gifts (1954). This shop still has no basement.

4 Edina Realty moved next door to this location in 1953 when Ruff Furs left, and it was there until 1961. Korst Jewelry shared space with them in 1953.

5 In 1942 there was an Edina Book Shop at the same address as the barber's. They advertised a rental library.

6 Edina Livery is listed in 1939 as connected with Bud Brook's Texaco at 54th and France and then as part of the Pure Oil station at 4045 France in 1942. In 1946, there was a second cab company, Edina Taxi, at 51st and Eden. In 1948, both companies seem to have merged at the Eden address under the name of Verlin Balfanz. He advertised delivery of packages and appliances. Meanwhile

50th Street looking east, December 18, 1941.

the address of 5020 France was occupied in 1948 by Eddie's Town and Country Service, which advertised lawn care and snow removal.

This building was built on the site of the Hartzell/Danens driveway after it had been filled in. See pages 14 and 106.

7 Early names were Edina Village Center (1941) and Edina Village Bowling Center (1943). In 1955 it had the name Edina Bowling Center.

8 This was called the Retail Lumbermen's Inter-Insurance Building.

9 His address was 5048 France, probably indicating the location of the house north of 5050, even though the curving driveway began south of 5050.

10 The 1944 occupant was B & B service, which advertised service of vacuum cleaners and appliances.

11 Hilma used the name Country Club Beauty Shop in 1939.

12 This was called Town and Country Cleaners.

13 The next pharmacist was Qualey. Current owner Del Nelson bought the property from Albert Nelson in 1972 and leased it to Pickwick Books in 1984. (Interview with Del Nelson, 1986.)

14 Albert Nelson built the building in 1923. (Interview with Rodney T. Nelson of Albert Lea, Minnesota, January 18, 1987.) According to current owner Del Nelson, this property has had such tenants as a chiropractor, Quality Book Store, McGarvey Coffee distributor, Robert's Formal Wear, and gift stores.

15 A second addition was built in 1987.

16 The Edina directory shows Karagheusian Rug Service in 1945 and Edina Electric at 4941 France in 1949, advertising appliances and repairs.

17 In a 1939 ad, Kountry Klub Karmelkorn advertised kandies and home cooking including chicken, steaks, chops, and donuts.

18 According to a 1942 ad, Zipoy's used this same lot at that time for customer parking.

19 Bachman's moved to this location in 1947. According to Barbara Dennison, this building faces the parking lot rather than France Avenue because it had first been designed to face Market Street on the Kallestad lot.

20 Barbara Dennison, daughter of Abdiel Kalestad, states that her father in the thirties had "a barn out back with a dozen chickens, some bees, and a cow. He would leave the cow in Baird's pasture, which is now White Oaks, when he went to work, and he called us to dinner with 'Dinner Call' on his bugle." She also remembers the Boogie Woogie records that she, her sister Virginia, and

The 50th Street location of Nolan's Cafe with Olson and Adolphson's grocery store, December 18, 1941.

their friends from Southwest High School would play after school while her mother Hilda took off her hearing aid. Many neighborhood teenagers would stay for dinner. But if the noise was too loud, their boarder, Emma Berg, would sit down at the grand piano and lead them in "He walks with me and he talks with me." (Interview, February 9, 1988.)

21 William A. Scott and Jeffrey A. Hess, *History and Architecture of Edina, Minnesota*, City of Edina, 1981, pp. 60–61 and Harold Sand interview, July 15, 1986.

22 The address here was either 4926 (1942, 1948) or 4928 (1947). In 1949, Ed Stow had a realty office in the basement space. When he moved out, he offered his safe to Bill Korst, Sr. who remembers rolling it down the sidewalk to his jewelry store where it still remains.

23 There were also apartments on the second floor.

24 This brick-front building was later called Hartzell Motors.

25 Some of the bakery names were: Sweetart Pastry Shop (1940), Filipek (1942), Mary Mac (1943), Heagle's (1943) and Gordie's (1957).

26 Hacken Mueller's Meat Market was added to Zipoy's in 1953. This name is variously spelled as one word with or without a hyphen.

27 The 1940 listing has the names Benson Shoe Repair and Edina Cleaners and Tailors. In 1947, Crown Cleaners shared the space with Graff's Edina Shoe Repair.

28 According to Bill Jordan, the closing of Doc's fountain caused a big reaction on the corner. Edina Historical Society has artifacts from this fountain service.

29 Various doctors over the years have had their offices above the pharmacy and barbershop. In 1940 it was Drs. Raymond Waters and R.W. Dowidat.

30 There was only one house on Gorgas before this date. The Kells and the Oxboroughs farmed the field between 50th and 49th with vegetables. (Interview with Barbara Dennison, February 20, 1988.)

31 Belleson's address in 1949 was 3912. In that same year, the 3906 tenant was Scott Stores, a variety store; at 3910 was Klad Ezee Children's Store. In 1948, Town and Country Hardware was opened at 3914 (*Southwest Shopper*, July 21, 1948) and expanded into 3916 in 1956. In 1960, 3906 was Ben Franklin and 3910 was Bermel-Smaby Realtors.

32 Hay and Stenson advertised a "nationally-known wine cellar." The business became the Edina Municipal Liquor Store in 1949.

33 The name used was Nolan's Golf Terrace Cafe.

50th Street looking west, ca. 1955.

34 Anbuhl, Inc., a ladies' "ready-to-wear" shop, seems to have replaced Adolphson & Olson in 1947, while Nolan's was next occupied in 1953 by W.R. Bliss and in 1959 by Nicollet Watches, Beeline Company and the Edina Cafeteria.

35 Herberger's was preceded in 1942 by Fabian's Women's Wearing Apparel and in 1943 by Helen Stevens' Women's Wearing Apparel. Herberger decided at this time to concentrate on small-town locations rather than to continue in the metropolitan area (*Minneapolis Star*, April 8, 1949).

36 This whole complex was referred to as the Edina Shopping Center or Gamble's Shopping Center: Gamble Stores, Keller Drug Co. and Herberger's Department Store. Their ad boasted "everything under one roof." The manager in 1948 was Roy Berg (*Southwest Shopper*, Sept. 1, 1948). Roy Clancy bought the drugstore from Keith Keller in 1949 and expanded into the Gamble's lower level in 1956 (*Minneapolis Star and Tribune*, July 24, 1986). Craftone Designs seems to have occupied the lower level in 1953.

37 The Edina Library opened in the fifty-year-old D.W. Wallace house, 4120 W. 50th St., in May of 1955. The library was a compromise use of the house in that it served as a buffer between residences and the new First Edina National Bank at 4100 W. 50th St. (*Minneapolis Star*, May 17, 1955.)

38 In 1940 this was called Borey's Service Station, and in 1948 it was called Hick's Shell Station.

39 The station owners are identified as Bud Brooks (1942) and Leroy Balfanz (1948).

40 Another house in this area with the address of 5043 France was occupied by the Oyers. There were also residences south of Sampson's house at 5021 and 5053/5055 Halifax at least as far back as 1940.

41 Barbara Dennison remembers this as Pulver's Drive-in. (Interview, February 20, 1988.)

42 National Tea was preceded at this location by the Edina Groceteria (1942).

43 The Krake house was closer to the present 3925 (Len Druskin) than to the present 3917. After this house was gone around 1950, Russ Lund built the present buildings whose first tenants in 1953 were Arthur Murray Studios, Brush's Shoes, Lillian's, Bettina Shakespeare and Dahl's.

44 The Brown Derby was operated by Bill and Lee Olson from 1934 to 1955 when it was sold for $7000 to Mr. and Mrs. Kermit Dahm. (Interview with Lee Olson, June 19, 1987.)

45 The addresses from 3913 to 3901 have changed both officially and unofficially over the years from 1936 to the present, a fact that makes identification difficult.

46 The earliest telephone listing for the west location is Town and Country Floral Shop in 1939. This was taken over by Bachman's as their first branch store in 1941. (*Purple Packages*; *Bachman's 100 years*, 1985, page 17.) After buying the west store in 1953, Ed Storm soon dropped the sporting goods in favor of art supplies. In 1965, he began his picture-framing business.

Two early establishments that were in either this location or at 3915 are the Country Club Associate Store in 1935 (E.J. Barry's Hardware and Sporting Goods) and the Edina Ice Cream Store in 1937. Their address is given simply as "Edina Theater Building."

47 The east store had the new women's wear tenants Bettina Shakespeare (1949) and The Norm (1953).

48 In 1949, Hasty-Tasty advertised homemade pastries. From 1939 to 1947, the establishment here was Hoyt's Cafe, which sold chow mein for take-out. According to Grace Hansen, the Hartzell garage was rebuilt and split into more than one shop after Hartzell moved to his France Avenue location around 1925.

49 In 1945, R.L. DeShane, Plumbers seems to have taken over this basement space.

50 B.A. Rose Music Store was at this location from 1963 to 1985.

51 Grace Hansen interview, June 26, 1987.

52 Information from interviews with William Korst, Sr. on January 31 and February 14, 1987.

Afterword

We used to have people around this corner, those guys I've told you about, that were real characters. Now that it's more built up, there aren't as many transients around here like Kent and Lamitz and Little Erick.

But people out here haven't changed that much in fifty years. Children have changed, though. You can almost tell the way they come into the barbershop and the way they handle themselves. In those days, they would do what you told 'em. If a kid was doin' something he shouldn't be doin' and you told 'im about it, he'd listen to you then. Nowadays, maybe not.

The real changes are the ones you see out in these neighborhoods. When I first came out here, for example, 48th and France, where Good Shepherd Church is, was a dump for clean fill — concrete blocks or whatever you had. Now, all these places are filled up. They keep putting up houses and other buildings. But I never, ever dreamt that this corner would become as big as it has. I knew it would grow some, but I didn't think it would grow this much!

I've had a good life, in the shop and at home. My wife, Wilma, was a cook at Wooddale School for many years, and we have three daughters, Phyllis, Vernice, and Kathy, and three grandsons and three granddaughters. Not one of them has caused me a minute's sorrow.

Being a barber has always been fascinating to me. I've never, ever seen the day when I hated to come to work. That's because I like people and I like the art of barbering, and I liked the art of shaving, too.

I give everybody the best I got. No one can ask for more than that.

Vern Swanson
June, 1986

Key to 1936 Drawing

1. Adams residence
2. Edina State Bank
3. Hay and Stenson Liquor
4. Kell residence
5. Oxborough residence
6. Peterson's Barber Shop
7. Gregg's Pharmacy
8. Benson Shoe Repair/Edina Cleaners and Tailors
9. Nelson Dry Goods
10. Olson's Grocery
11. Adolphson's Meat Market
12. Edina Hardware Store
13. Sweetart Pastry Shop (1940)
14. Hartzell's Edina Garage
15. Village Inn
16. residence (Trinity Chapel, 1872)
17. Hartzell's Used Car Lot
18. Kountry Klub Karmelkorn restaurant
19. Gambles (ca. 1941)
20. Country Club Standard Service
21. Piggly Wiggly Grocery
22. Texaco Oil Service
23. Pulver's root beer stand
24. Sampson residence
25. Oyer residence
26. Moe/Gaulke residence
27. Krake residence
28. Brown Derby Cafe
29. Edina Theatre
30. theatre parking lot
31. Town and Country Florists (1939)
32. Anthonie Frock Shop
33. Hoyt's Cafe (1939)
34. Brauer's 5¢ to $1.00 Store/ Danen Construction (1940)
35. France Avenue Beauty Shop
36. Edina Realty (1939)
37. Nolan's Cafe
38. Forberg's Ice Cream Co.
39. Lindquist blacksmith
40. Nelson's Rexall Drug
41. Knutson and Turner's Red and White Grocery
42. Thompson Lumber
43. Perl Lotion
44. Hilma's Beauty Shop
45. Bert's Barber Shop
46. Gus the plumber
47. Creimen's Restaurant and Beer Parlor
48. residence
49. residence
50. residence

Dates in parentheses indicate the earliest known tenants of shops that existed in 1936.

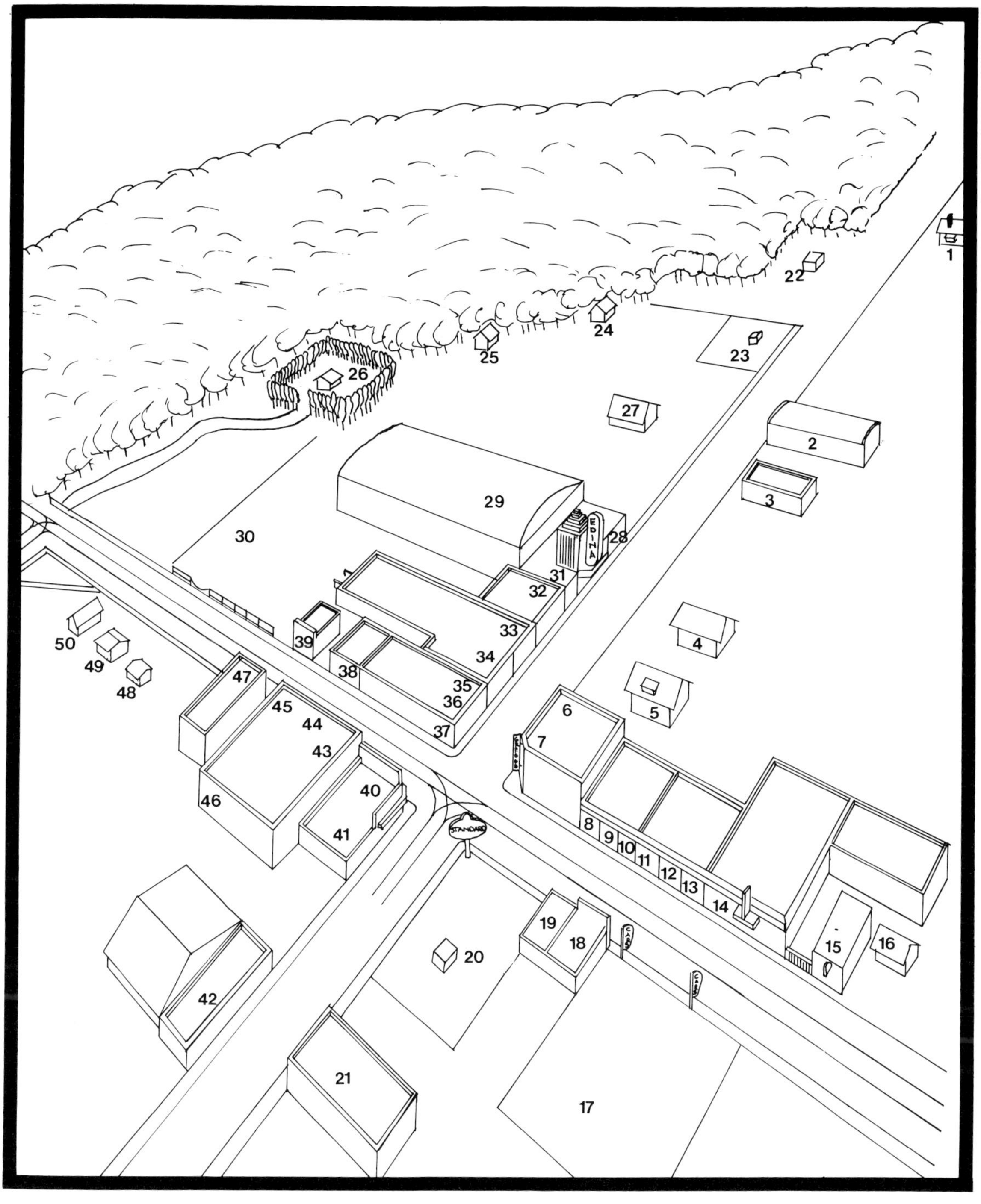
1
22
23
24
25
26
27
2
3
29
30
EDINA
28
31
32
33
34
35
36
37
38
39
4
5
6
7
47
45
44
43
46
40
41
STANDARD
50
49
48
8
9
10
11
12
13
14
15
16
19
18
20
42
21
17